Falling in Love with Jesus
Workbook

BY DEE BRESTIN AND KATHY TROCCOLI

THOMAS NELSON
Since 1798

NASHVILLE   DALLAS   MEXICO CITY   RIO DE JANEIRO

Published in Nashville, Tennessee, by Thomas Nelson. Thomas Nelson is a registered trademark of Thomas Nelson, Inc.

Thomas Nelson, Inc., titles may be purchased in bulk for educational, business, fund-raising, or sales promotional use. For information, please e-mail SpecialMarkets@ThomasNelson.com.

Unless otherwise indicated, Scripture quotations used in this book are from The Holy Bible, New International Version. © 1973, 1978, 1984, International Bible Society. Used by permission of Zondervan Bible Publishers.

Other Scripture references are from the following sources:

The Amplified Bible: Old Testament (AMP), © 1962, 1964 by Zondervan Publishing House; and the Amplified New Testament, © 1958 by the Lockman Foundation. Used by permission.

The King James Version of the Bible (KJV).

The New King James Version (NKJV), © 1979, 1980, 1982, 1992, Thomas Nelson, Inc., Publisher.

J. B. Phillips: The New Testament in Modern English, Revised Edition (PHILLIPS). © J. B. Phillips 1958, 1960, 1972. Used by permission of Macmillan Publishing Co., Inc.

The Message (MSG), © 1993. Used by permission of NavPress Publishing Group.

The Living Bible (TLB), © 1971 by Tyndale House Publishers, Wheaton, Ill. Used by permission.

The New Revised Standard Version Bible (NRS), © 1989 by the Division of Christian Education of the National Council of the Churches of Christ in the United States of America. Used by permission.

ISBN 978-0-8499-8821-9

Library of Congress Cataloging-in-Publication Data available

Printed in the United States of America
HB 09.30.2022

To the Beloved of Christ,
you dear precious women whom we
have the privilege of speaking to, singing to,
writing for, and praying over.

You are the object of His affection.

Acknowledgments

To the Thomas Nelson team:
We thank each member at Thomas Nelson who has contributed to this endeavor.
We especially thank:

Mark Sweeney, David Moberg, and Lee Gessner—for believing in us,
listening to us, and catching the excitement for what this could mean
in the lives of women.

Ami McConnell and Kathy Decker—for your enthusiasm, and for editing
with great sensitivity.

Harry Clayton, Heidi Groff, and Russ Hall—for your commitment to
excellence, in being sensitive to capture the unique and passionate
content of the book on video.

Debbie Wickwire—you are far more than an author liaison—you are a
friend who is indeed respected deeply. How kind of God to have you
involved in this project.

To our team:
Matt and Steve—for constantly being men of integrity. It feels so safe to
know that you always want to be sensitive to what God desires.

Our faithful prayer teams—for your willingness to place yourself at the feet
of Jesus on our behalf.

Linda and Gay—you are priceless.

Dee—
This has been such a beautiful experience for me. You have become a cherished
mentor. Thank you for pursuing me, encouraging me, and teaching me. I love you.

Kath

Kathy—
Thank you for saying yes, yes, yes . . . to the book, the video, the friendship. How
thankful I am to you for being so vulnerable, so fun, so honest, so passionate . . .
How amazing it has been to see the glory of God fall. I love you.

Dee

Contents

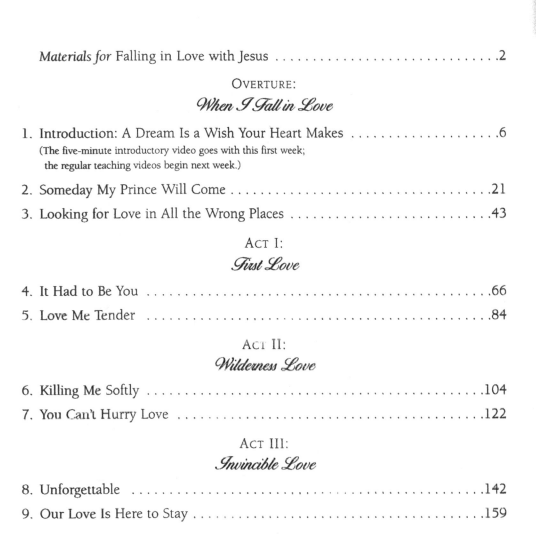

Stop!
In the Name of Love

If you are not in a deep love relationship and feel like flipping the switch when the topics of romance, weddings, and marriage come up—*don't!* Though love songs will be sung and romantic stories told, we are using these as "parables" to help you understand the best romance, which is your relationship with Jesus, who is the ultimate Bridegroom for all believing women, whether they are single or married.

We pray this won't be just a sentimental journey, but a journey that you can look back on and say: "It was during those ten weeks that I began to really see Jesus in a new way and yearn for an intimacy with Him that I had not known."

Please remember, you are His Beloved. You are the object of His affection. He wants to whisper words of love to you. He wants to take you higher, out of the hiding places, into the land of invincible love.

If you are thinking, *I don't know if I even want a deep love relationship with Jesus. I feel dead inside,* hang on! You may feel skeptical, but we plead with you to keep your heart open. You may discover the greatest romance of your life.

Materials for Falling in Love with Jesus

THE BIBLE STUDY WORKBOOK (CAN BE PURCHASED INDIVIDUALLY)
The Workbook you are holding is an in-depth Bible study. It contains ten lessons, each divided into five days. Plan to spend at least thirty minutes each day alone with Jesus.

All you *must* have for the study is this Workbook and a Bible. It can be done on your own without watching the video or meeting with a small group of women. However, we so encourage you to seek out women who desire a more intimate relationship with Jesus. Just as "the daughters of Jerusalem" in the Song of Songs encouraged the bride in her love for the bridegroom, so will your sisters in Christ encourage you. If you are doing this in a group, one woman (or you can take turns) should be the discussion facilitator, using the Leader's Guide included in the Leader's Packet.

THE LEADER'S PACKET CONTAINS:

- One Workbook
- One Leader's Guide
- One Video Teaching Set
- One Book

WHAT CAN I EXPECT IN THE VIDEO TEACHING SET?
The Video Teaching Set consists of ten videos with lessons that correspond with the Workbook. Each week you will come together, watch that week's video, then discuss the corresponding lesson in the Workbook. The first video is a five-minute introduction. Videos two through nine are approximately thirty minutes in length. The review week does not include a video portion. We have purposely kept the video portion brief to give you time to share what the Lord has taught you during the week. We've seen tremendous growth occur when women are faithful in doing their homework, faithful in keeping confidences, and courageous enough to be honest with God and with one another. The videos are meant to be a catalyst both for understanding God's Word and for honesty. In the videos you will see:

1. Strong teaching from Dee
2. Poignant sharing in story and song from Kathy

MUST I PURCHASE THE BOOK, *FALLING IN LOVE WITH JESUS,* AS WELL AS THIS WORKBOOK?

No. Essential excerpts from the Book are in this Workbook, so you do not need the Book. However, you may choose to read the Book as well, not only because you may find it enjoyable, but also because relating to Jesus as your Bridegroom may be new for you, and the review would be helpful.

WHERE CAN I PURCHASE MATERIALS?

Your local Christian bookstore or any of the following Web sites:

www.deebrestin.com
www.troccoli.com
www.Christianbook.com
www.amazon.com
www.bn.com

OVERTURE

When I Fall in Love

∽

Orchestra
maestoso e appassionato
(Begin strongly, with majesty, to stir the heart)

Introduction: A Dream Is a Wish Your Heart Makes

Prelude

Do you know the secret of overcoming a hundred sins in your life? Of having an inextinguishable joy—no matter the circumstances? It is a secret most believers have missed.

The secret lies not in ten steps, not in approaching the Bible as a self-improvement guide, but in being deeply in love with Jesus, so that your desire is to be completely abandoned to Him and to receive whatever He has for you. Those who learn to relate to Jesus as the Love of their life, on a moment-to-moment basis, have a vitality surpassing that of most believers and a victory over sins that once imprisoned them. Learning to approach Jesus as your Bridegroom may sound foreign to you, but it is a language you, as a woman, were designed to understand.

The metaphor of God as our Father is precious and valuable, but it is also vital to understand that Jesus is our Bridegroom. How wonderful to realize that we are cherished as a bride is cherished. We are the object of His affection.

Romantic love is unique in that it asks the beloved to forsake all others. The God who made us is lonely for us, desires to be with us, and is grieved when we try to fill the emptiness in our soul with loves other than Him. How intriguing that our awesome God longs for us to love Him in return—deeply, passionately, and with abandonment.

This week you will be getting an overview of the portrait God paints throughout Scripture of the intimate relationship He longs to have with you. He is the Bridegroom who woos, wins, and weds. He also intended earthly marriage to be a picture of this deeper reality. God planned for marriage and the marriage bed to be beautiful and undefiled. The world has dumped a garbage load of trash on the pure white sheets. But as it was originally planned, marriage has a spiritual parallel: the believer's relationship with Jesus, the ultimate Bridegroom. Throughout Scripture, as in Hosea, the Song of Songs, and Ephesians, God makes the parallel to an earthly love relationship to help us understand not only how He loves us but also how He longs for us to love Him.

Some of you may feel discomfort with this subject because you do not have or even yearn for a deep love relationship with Jesus. Perhaps your love for Jesus is conceptual, rather than actual. One young woman said, after she heard us speak on this subject, "This is so new to me. I have always known that Jesus loved me, but I never thought about Him longing for me to love Him back!"

There are also many believers who do understand passion for Jesus. Initially, they were enthralled with Him, but sadly the honeymoon is long gone and the mundaneness of life has caused their hearts to grow cold. They are sleeping beneath a blanket of deadness and cannot hear the call of God that says, "Awaken, Dear One, and come higher with Me."

This study may be fun for some of you, like the joyful wedding where Jesus turned water into wine; yet it is also solemn and sacred, just as when vows were exchanged on that day. Just as too many couples settle for a ho-hum marriage, too many believers settle for a ho-hum relationship with Jesus. Just as a good marriage takes work, so does a deep love relationship with Jesus. But, oh the rewards! We pray therefore that you will prepare your lesson carefully each week.

The study is divided into five days for five quiet times with the Lord. If you miss a day, don't get discouraged. Just go on and do the next day. At the end of the week, if time permits, make up any days you might have missed. We pray that your quiet time with the Lord will become a time you will begin to anticipate eagerly because you are receiving kisses from the King. (A kiss from the King, according to rabbinical tradition, is a living word from Scripture. When a verse leaps out at you and you have the sense that God has spoken personally to you, you have been kissed by the King.) When you are faithful in spending time with Jesus during the week, you will come to the discussion time glowing with excitement, and it will be contagious. Together, you will help one another fall more deeply in love with Jesus.

If you purchased this Workbook before your first meeting with other women, please do your lesson ahead of time. If you are a beginner to Bible study, you may find some of the questions challenging. Don't worry! You will get help when you get to the group meeting. What you may not realize is how very welcome you are—your newness adds a fresh enthusiasm that recharges those who have known the Lord a long time. *Everyone* has much to contribute.

The following additional materials will also deepen your love relationship with Jesus:

Appendix A: Song Lyrics
Lyrics from much-loved praise choruses and hymns are provided. We encourage you to turn there in your time alone with God and sing to Him or meditate on the words. Not only will this stir your heart to love Him more, it will bring great joy to your Lord. He delights in your praise.

Appendix B: Memory Verses
The power to change our lives lies in the very words of God. Keep

your heart open to memorizing Scripture. Copy the memory verse (or verses) for the week and place them on your refrigerator or mirror. We've chosen short verses that are easily learned, especially when kept in front of you. You'll be amazed at how easy memorizing Scripture is, and how much it impacts you.

Appendix C: Kisses from the King

Each time you meet with Jesus, ask Him to speak to you. Anticipate His kisses. Be ready to highlight anything in the text or Scripture that ministers to you. These pages are provided so you can record those kisses. Scripture is clear that one of the reasons we have a tendency to drift away from God is because we forget how good He has been to us. Keeping a record of His kisses will help you remember His tender mercies toward you.

Appendix D: Movie Night

Plans and discussion questions for Lerner and Loewe's classic musical *Camelot* are provided here. We encourage a group movie night, not only because it will promote bonding, but also because it will provide a model for how to see a secular story through spiritual eyes.

WATCH VIDEO #1: THE INTRODUCTORY VIDEO

After the video, put your chairs in as small a circle as possible for your discussion. (Space inhibits sharing.) If you are doing this lesson in a group, read the text and verses out loud. Begin with this week's Prelude.

If you did not get your Workbook before this first meeting, you can do it together now with the other women.

Getting to Know You

What interests you about this study? (Hear from a few.)

_____

_____

Share your name and a little about yourself to help the group get to know you. Name a favorite romantic song. Hear from everyone briefly.

_____

_____

In the video, what are some of the differences you noticed between Dee and Kathy?

_____

_____

What differences might there be among the women in your small group? How could these differences make this a stronger study?

_____

_____

What might a married woman learn from a single woman relating to Jesus as her Bridegroom? What might a single woman learn from a married woman concerning marriage being a metaphor for our relationship with Jesus?

_____

_____

Some groups *particularly* spur you on to a deeper love relationship with Jesus. How can you, as an individual, prepare and share so as to make this group the best it can be?

_____

_____

DAY 1

Love Is a Many Splendored Thing

Women are energized by romance, and mysterious truths become clear when spoken in our language. And when we realize just how tenderly Jesus loves us, an amazing power in us is unleashed. That's what we hope will happen to you as you do this study.

The prophets often compare our relationship with the Lord to the relationship of a bride with her bridegroom. Through Hosea the Lord says:

> *I will betroth you to me forever;*
> *I will betroth you in righteousness and justice,*
> *in love and compassion.* (Hosea 2:19)

And Isaiah tells us:

As a bridegroom rejoices over his bride,
  so will your God rejoice over you. (Isaiah 62:5b)

(The verse from Isaiah is your memory verse for this week. Tear it out from Appendix B and place it on your refrigerator, mirror, or dashboard.)

The Song of Songs also compares our relationship with the Lord to the relationship of a bride with her bridegroom. The Shulammite maiden in the Song of Songs represents you, and it will thrill your soul as you discover just how much Jesus loves you. If you have put your trust in Him, you are His Bride, His Beloved, and He looks at you with the same adoring eyes that Solomon, the earthly bridegroom, looked at the Shulammite maiden. And the same purity, faithfulness, and abandonment Solomon desired from the Shulammite maiden, Jesus desires from you.

We understand that sometimes the Song of Songs and the subjects of romance can make single women want to flip the switch. Kathy says, "We're tired of books and sermons on marriage, and of pastors who drone on and on about what a wife or husband should do and then, like an afterthought, tack on a sentence for single people at the end. They'll close their Bible, and in a deep pastoral voice, say: 'And for those of you who are single, just remember, as you leave today, keep Jesus as your Bridegroom.' At that point I think, *Hey, I live there. Every day, that's who Jesus is to me. But aren't we all supposed to live there? Why wasn't that comment included when you addressed the married couples?*"

In this Workbook we will learn *how to live there*, how to relate to Jesus as our Bridegroom.

1. How would you summarize this week's Prelude in one sentence?

   _____

   _____

2. Have you ever fallen in love? If so, describe what you were experiencing at that time.

   _____

   _____

   How does it make you feel to know God loves you like that?

   _____

   _____

3. On the metaphorical level of the Song of Songs, the Shulammite maiden represents us, and Solomon represents Jesus. In the following passages, what do you learn about how Jesus sees you and what He desires from you?

A. My lover spoke and said to me,
    "Arise, my darling,
    my beautiful one, and come with me." (Song of Songs 2:10)

_____

_____

B. My dove in the clefts of the rock,
      in the hiding places on the mountainside,
    show me your face,
      let me hear your voice;
    for your voice is sweet,
      and your face is lovely. (Song of Songs 2:14)

_____

_____

4. List all the ways, according to the following passage in Zephaniah, that God demonstrates His love toward us. Have you experienced any of the last three ways personally? If so, describe the time when you sensed this love.

   The LORD your God is with you,
     he is mighty to save.
   He will take great delight in you,
     he will quiet you with his love,
     he will rejoice over you with singing. (Zephaniah 3:17)

_____

_____

5. How does Isaiah describe God's love for us in the following passage (this week's
   memory verse)? What pictures does this bring to mind?

   As a bridegroom rejoices over his bride,
     so will your God rejoice over you. (Isaiah 62:5b)

_____

_____

The context leading to the above memory verse is interesting. Read it carefully:

No longer will they call you Deserted,
  or name your land Desolate.

But you will be called Hephzibah,
  and your land Beulah;
for the LORD will take delight in you,
  and your land will be married. (Isaiah 62:4)

In talking about God's people, Isaiah uses the image of a wife who has felt forsaken but is now restored. The neighbors of Israel had been speaking derisively of them, questioning, "Where is your God?" The word translated "Deserted" usually refers to being forsaken by a husband. The word *Hephzibah* means "My delight is in her." The word *Beulah* means "married." John Watts, in the *Word Biblical Commentary*, explains:

> The cutting remarks, like those to an abandoned wife or an unmarried woman, are silenced as she proudly wears her wedding ring and married name.[1]

Jesus delights in you. He longs to take you out of the hiding places and higher with Him. You are His Beloved.

DAY 2

Only You

Romantic love is different than other kinds of love because it demands faithfulness; it demands that you cleave to your "husband" and forsake all others. One of the reasons it is so important to God that the marriage bed be kept pure, that husbands and wives be faithful to one another, is because marriage is a picture of our relationship with Jesus.

Just as it is healthy for a husband and wife to be devoted to each other and to forsake all others, it is good for us to love Jesus with our whole hearts. It is dangerous when we allow our hearts to run after other gods, whatever those may be in our lives (a consuming career, a secret sin, another person, a false god). Philip Yancey writes: "The words of the prophets sound like the words of a lover's quarrel drifting through thin apartment walls."[2] In fact, the whole Book of Hosea is a parable showing God's heartbreak. Despite His great kindness to us, we have gone running after false lovers. The other prophets echo this lament.

Spend some time memorizing your verse. Often taking a word at a time helps you cement it in your memory:

Isaiah
     Isaiah 62
          Isaiah 62:5
               Isaiah 62:5 As
                    Isaiah 62:5 As a
                         Isaiah 62:5 As a bridegroom . . .

6. In the following passages, how does God describe the unfaithfulness of His people? What do you learn from the word picture given in each?

   A. *What can I do with you, Ephraim?*
      What can I do with you, Judah?
      Your love is like the morning mist,
         like the early dew that disappears. (Hosea 6:4)

   _____

   _____

   B. *How can you say, "I am not defiled;*
      I have not run after the Baals"?
      See how you behaved in the valley;
         consider what you have done.
      You are a swift she-camel
         running here and there,
      a wild donkey accustomed to the desert,
         sniffing the wind in her craving—
         in her heat who can restrain her?
      Any males that pursue her need not tire themselves;
         at mating time they will find her.
      Do not run until your feet are bare
         and your throat is dry.
      But you said, "It's no use!
         I love foreign gods,
         and I must go after them." (Jeremiah 2:23–25)

   _____

   _____

7. Can you identify with either of the above pictures? How has your love for the Lord been like a "morning mist"? When have you behaved like a "she-camel"? How has this behavior hurt you?

   _____

   _____

8. Our unfaithfulness to the Lord not only hurts Him, it puts us in great danger. Paul often expresses this concept through the parable of marriage in the New Testament. When we fail to trust our "husband," Christ, we open ourselves up to deception. How is this explained in the following passage?

> I am jealous for you with a godly jealousy. I promised you to one husband, to Christ, so that I might present you as a pure virgin to him. But I am afraid that just as Eve was deceived by the serpent's cunning, your minds may somehow be led astray from your sincere and pure devotion to Christ. (2 Corinthians 11:2–3)

_____

_____

9. Despite our unfaithfulness, God is faithful. What do you learn about God's love from the following word pictures?

A. The LORD said to me, "Go, show your love to your wife again, though she is loved by another and is an adulteress. Love her as the LORD loves the Israelites, though they turn to other gods and love the sacred raisin cakes." (Hosea 3:1)

_____

_____

B. As surely as the sun rises,
   he will appear;
he will come to us like the winter rains,
   like the spring rains that water the earth. (Hosea 6:3b)

_____

_____

C. Because of the LORD's great
love we are not consumed,
   for his compassions never fail.
They are new every morning;
   great is your faithfulness. (Lamentations 3:22–23)

_____

_____

10. In doing this study, what are some ways you could demonstrate faithfulness to the Lord, in the same way that He is faithful to you?

_____

_____

How to Handle a Woman

When Cinderella sings "A Dream Is a Wish Your Heart Makes," females from nine to ninety sigh. God knows us, He designed us to be uniquely feminine, and He knows how to talk to us. Each morning He says, "Good morning, Princess" when He causes the sun to rise, and each evening, He says, "Good night, My Beloved" as the sun goes down. Continually, He makes a romantic analogy in Scripture, telling us that He is our heavenly Bridegroom. In the musical *Camelot*, King Arthur sings "How to Handle a Woman." A wise old man told him the secret, a secret known to every woman. What is it?

It is to love her. Simply love her.

As a member of the relational sex, we long to be loved, we long to be cherished. And we are very interested in romance, in stories in which the hero deeply loves and sacrifices for the lady. God knows this, for He made us.

Intriguingly, when God instructs earthly husbands how to treat their wives, He doesn't recommend that they order them around, or post signs declaring that they are the king of the castle. (There is great ironic humor in the opening of the Book of Esther when husbands tried to do exactly that.) Instead, God instructs a spirit of sacrificial servant love:

> *Husbands, love your wives, just as Christ loved the church and gave himself up for her to make her holy, cleansing her by the washing with water through the word, and to present her to himself as a radiant church, without stain or wrinkle or any other blemish, but holy and blameless. In this same way, husbands ought to love their wives as their own bodies.* (Ephesians 5:25–29)

11. Describe a time when a man treated you tenderly. How does it make you feel to know that Jesus wants to treat you with that same tenderness?

_____

_____

12. In one sentence, describe a time when you were aware of God's tenderness to you.

_____

_____

In your time with God, ask Him to tenderly guide you, opening your eyes to new insights.

13. Whether you are single or married, if you have put your trust in Christ, He is your husband. Meditate on the following passages from Isaiah. What do you learn from each concerning God's love for you?

A. *For your Maker is your husband—*
    the LORD Almighty is his name. (Isaiah 54:5)

_____

_____

B. *I delight greatly in the LORD;*
    my soul rejoices in my God.
  For he has clothed me with garments of salvation
    and arrayed me in a robe of righteousness,
  as a bridegroom adorns his head like a priest,
    and as a bride adorns herself with her jewels. (Isaiah 61:10)

_____

_____

14. How did Jesus, like the hero in a great romance, deeply sacrifice for you?

_____

_____

15. What are some of the prisons from which He has rescued you?

_____

_____

That's the Story of Love

In considering how to draw closer to Jesus, my heavenly Bridegroom, I can draw upon what I (Dee) have learned from my earthly marriage to Steve. Our marriage has progressed through three stages:

1. FIRST LOVE
2. WILDERNESS LOVE
3. INVINCIBLE LOVE

Most marriages never make it to the third stage. Though couples may manage to stay married, they do not arrive at invincible love. After the exciting time of first love, they get lost in the wilderness. You see these couples in restaurants, consumed with their linguini rather than their love. The tender glances, the laughter, the *romance* is gone. They may have moments of intimacy together, but basically, those moments are just an occasional rendezvous in the desert.

But there *are* couples who are attentive enough to God to find their way out of the wilderness into the promised land of invincible love. This is absolutely the sweetest place on earth. Because of God's grace, Steve and I are experiencing this. As in our wonderful first-love stage, we are eager to be together, and each of us lights up when the other walks in the room. But this third stage is deeper, and far better. There is a great joy in knowing and being known, and in the security that our love, no matter what, is here to stay.

The same three stages are true in a believer's relationship to Jesus. Most believers, sadly, never make it to the third stage. They love the Lord, and they have times of intimacy with Him, but basically their lives are devoid of passion for Him. They are simply having an occasional rendezvous in the wilderness with Him.

Though we will refer to many scriptural models, our primary model will be Mary of Bethany.

16. In one sentence, describe Mary in each of the following stages in her love relationship with Jesus:

    A. First Love (Luke 10:38–39): _____

    _____

    B. Wilderness Love (John 11:5–6): _____

C. Invincible Love (John 12:1–3): _____

_____

More challenging passages can be found in the Song of Songs, but the same pattern is repeated. When there is an important truth in Scripture, you will find it in more than one place. Just as Mary of Bethany went through three stages, so did the Shulammite maiden.

17. In one sentence, describe the Shulammite maiden in each of the following stages in her love relationship with Solomon:

A. First Love (Song of Songs 1:2): _____

_____

Just as the Shulammite eagerly desired Solomon's kisses in her first-love time, so should we desire kisses from the King. When a verse leaps out at you, giving you exactly what you needed, you have been "kissed by the King." We'll learn more about the kisses of the King, but for now, be alert to how He may kiss you through His Word. When that happens, be sure to highlight it. If you are comfortable writing in your Bible, write in the margin the date and how the verse ministered to you. You may also record His kisses in the back of this workbook (see Appendix C).

B. Wilderness Love (Song of Songs 3:1–2): _____

_____

Though we will look at the context of this passage more deeply later, it is important to realize that in the preceding chapter, the lover asked the beloved to go higher with him, and she refused. She stayed in the "hiding places." So he has left her and gone higher alone. However, eventually she *does* go higher with him, and that leads her into the land of invincible love, where nothing, absolutely nothing, can quench her love.

C. Invincible Love (Song of Songs 8:6–7a): _____

_____

As you spend time with God, ask Him to give you confidence that you are His Beloved.

A Dream Is a Wish Your Heart Makes

Author Mary Blye Howe writes:

> God is a being who thirsts for us individually, who loves us to distraction and who will stop at nothing to gain our love in return. Like a lover, God sees each of us as uniquely beautiful. Lovers are consumed by desire, wanting just to be near one another. They lie awake thinking of the one they love, examining new ideas that might win their love, counting the days when they'll be near that person again. Lovers are infatuated, a word that my dictionary defines as an "extravagant love or desire marked by a strong attachment and unreasoning love." How lovely![3]

Do you have trouble believing that God loves you this much?

You are not alone. God is so holy, so magnificent, so perfect. When we first become aware of the holiness of God, we feel so unworthy. We shrink from such perfection; we are aware that His holy light has illumined all our blemishes.

Many believers from the past have experienced the feeling that Jesus could not possibly love them, for they recognized their unworthiness. But then! They experienced the wonder of assurance. John Wesley wrote "And Can It Be?" Likewise, former slave trader John Newton wrote the song that has become a favorite, "Amazing Grace." (You can sing or meditate on the lyrics of those songs given in Appendix A.)

18. Do you have trouble believing Jesus loves you and actually delights in you? Why or why not?

_____

_____

19. In the following passages, note how the "beloved" felt when she or he first became aware of the love of Jesus (Jesus is hidden in these passages in the figures of Boaz, David, and Solomon):

A. Ruth 2:8–10 _____

_____

B. 2 Samuel 9:6–8 _____

C. Song of Songs 1:6 _____

_____

D. Luke 5:4–8 _____

_____

You, too, may find it hard to believe that someone as powerful, as wonderful, and as pure as Jesus loves you. But He does. "God loves you just the way you are," as Max Lucado says, "but he refuses to leave you that way."[4] He is on a quest to bring you higher. Each of the above individuals eventually became confident of the love of God for them—and that can happen for you as well.

Even if God never gives you an earthly Prince Charming, or turns your husband into one, you have a Prince who is wonderful. Our God is so much more amazing than even our idea of Prince Charming. He is perfect, His love never fails, He is omnipotent, and best of all, He is *not* just some historical figure from the past—He is alive today. Peter puts it like this:

> *For we have not been telling you fairy tales when we explained to you the power of our Lord Jesus Christ and his coming again. My own eyes have seen his splendor and his glory.* (2 Peter 1:16 TLB)

Dream big. Pray hard. Jesus *is* our Prince, and He is no fairy tale.

Finale

REVIEW
20. Each woman should share, if she chooses, one thing that God impressed on her heart from this study, one way she was "kissed by the King."

_____

_____

PRAYER
Close in silent prayer today. Each woman should pray, silently, that the woman on her right will fall more deeply in love with Jesus. The discussion facilitator will close in audible prayer.

Someday My Prince Will Come

Prelude

When Snow White sings "Someday My Prince Will Come," she isn't dreaming of a guy who will love her and leave her. She wants a genuine Prince Charming, a man of character, someone who will never forsake her and who will whisk her off into the happily ever after.

Likewise, Kathy dreams of a man of character—an amazing man with a deep connection to God, a man of intelligence, sensitivity, and charisma. In 1994, she began keeping a journal to the man she prays will one day be her husband. When she vulnerably brought out her journal and showed it to me, I could see a marvelous parallel. Just as women long for a wonderful earthly bridegroom, there is a part in each of us, whether we realize it or not, that God has created to yearn for our heavenly Bridegroom.

On an autumn night, Kathy began her journal.

October 20, 1994 10:15 P.M.

I can't believe I'm finally doing this . . . actually putting my pen to the paper and writing my heart to you . . . you . . . by the time I read this out loud—you'll be here—I'll see your eyes, I'll feel your hair, I'll touch your strong hands, and hear the sound of the voice I'll hear for a lifetime—the voice I've been longing to hear—the voice that will ignite me, soothe me, speak passionately to me . . .

I wonder where you are tonight—I've been praying for you—I wonder if you're yearning for me too . . . Please know I long to hold you, kiss you, share the depths of my soul with you . . . Sweet man of my heart—I go to bed this night with the comfort of knowing you're out there—and the hope that someday we will be together.

I want to dream with you—drink life with you—journey to high places with you.

Please find me.

Just as God has put within the heart of each of us a yearning to be a bride, He has also given us a yearning for a bridegroom who is *wonderful*. Not only do Kathy's journal entries pulse with longing, they show the kind of husband that each of us, in our deepest of hearts, desires.

December 22, 1994 9:30 A.M.

> *Almost Christmas . . . just spent a little time in prayer. Once again, I think of you—I pray that you will grow strong with God yet have His sweet tenderness . . . I pray that you will know me—really know me—and be able to look in my eyes, and read the pulse of my heart. I pray that you will take me far into a "once upon a time."*
> *Come soon, dear one . . . I wait . . .*

Wonderful men *do* exist, outside of fairy tales, because of the power of Christ. But even if a man like this never comes to sweep you off your feet, even if your husband never surrenders to the power of Christ and becomes a veritable Prince Charming, there is One who is definitely coming. He is going to carry you away, if, through the grace of God, you have put your trust in Him. He is tender and strong, He knows you—really knows you—and He will take you, if you have put your trust in Him, far into a place so beautiful that your finite mind cannot even imagine it. Your wedding day is coming. The apostle John was given a vision in the last book of the Bible, a vision of a day that is really coming:

> *Let us rejoice and be glad*
> *and give him glory!*
> *For the wedding of the Lamb has come,*
> *and his bride has made herself ready.* (Revelation 19:7)

Do you know who the Lamb is? It is Jesus. Precious Jesus. And never was there a Bridegroom like Him.

He created the world for you, left His Father's throne for you, endured the cross for you, and rose from the dead to be your Living Savior, your Good Shepherd, your Omnipotent Lord. He sees your heartache and tears, understands your deepest longings, knows, better than you do, what you need, and has the power to help you. How clearly this is demonstrated in this week's story.

Luke alone records the birth story of our Lord. Many believe that Luke's primary sources were the women who traveled with Jesus, making him the Gospel writer most empathetic to women. It is Luke who gives us a good look at the hearts and lives of Elizabeth, the mother of John the Baptist, and Mary, the mother of Jesus.

Though these women ushered in the birth of Jesus, He existed before they did. He simply came to earth at Christmas, taking on the form of a baby. Poet Luci Shaw describes this amazing paradox as "infinity walled in a womb," as "the Word, stern-sentenced to be nine months dumb."[1] Jesus has always existed. He created Elizabeth.

ANDREA DEL SARTO (1486–1530)[1]

༄

We don't know if Mary and Elizabeth were actually together after the birth of Jesus, but they may have been. We know the bond between the two women was close, as was the bond between Jesus and John the Baptist, and we believe the artist has captured that intimacy in many ways. Zechariah is the background. We believe that the marriage of Elizabeth and Zechariah was a helpful mentoring model for Mary and Joseph.

He even created His own mother. John the Apostle explains how Jesus has always existed, how He made the world:

> *Through him all things were made; without him nothing was made that has been made.* (John 1:3)

Not only did Jesus create Elizabeth and Mary, He was mindful of them. He knew their needs better than they did, and He found ways to meet those needs. As you listen to Dee tell their story today, remember that Jesus was not only mindful of Elizabeth and Mary, He is mindful of you. He is the perfect husband. He knows you—really knows you. He provides for you, protects you, and can read the pulse of your heart.

WATCH VIDEO #2: SOMEDAY MY PRINCE WILL COME

As you listen to the story of Elizabeth and Mary, we want to free you *not* to take notes. In *The Divine Conspiracy*, Dallas Willard observed:

> The teacher in Jesus' time—and especially the religious teacher—taught in such a way that he would impact the life flow of the hearer, leaving a lasting impression without benefit of notes, recorders, or even memorization. Whatever did not make a difference in that way just made no difference.[2]

That is not to say that there is not value in taking notes, and of course, if you want to jot something down, please do, and the following space is provided for that. But because Dee is teaching from a narrative passage, telling you a story, you might learn best by simply watching and listening intently. This is also true of subsequent videos in this series.

The story Dee will be telling begins in Luke 1:6. Open your Bible to that passage in case you want to refer to the story.

_____

_____

_____

_____

_____

_____

_____

_____

GROUP RESPONSE TO THE VIDEO

Hear from a few women for each question. (If you are naturally talkative, share, but hold back for the shyer members by sharing just once. If you are naturally shy, ask God to give you the courage to speak up when you have something to contribute.)

A. What are some ways that God cared for Elizabeth? For Mary?
B. What impact did the teaching in this video have on you personally, and why?
C. How could you apply this to your life?

DAY 1

Anticipation

The Book of Ecclesiastes tells us that, within each of us, God placed a longing—a longing for eternity, a longing for Him:

> *He has made everything beautiful in its time. He has also set eternity in the hearts of men.* (Ecclesiastes 3:11)

Authors Brent Curtis and John Eldredge describe, in *The Sacred Romance*, how having "eternity in our hearts" affects us, from the time we are small:

> A Sacred Romance calls to us through our heart every moment of our lives. It whispers to us on the wind, invites us through the laughter of good friends, reaches out to us through the touch of someone we love. We've

heard it in our favorite music, sensed it at the birth of our first child, been drawn to it while watching the shimmer of a sunset on the ocean. The Romance is even present in times of great personal suffering: the illness of a child, the loss of a marriage, the death of a friend. Something calls to us through experiences like these and rouses an inconsolable longing deep within our heart, wakening in us a yearning for intimacy, beauty, and adventure.[3]

Consider the ways God has been calling to you from the time you were small. Begin memorizing this week's memory verse (see Appendix B).

> The LORD your God is with you,
>   he is mighty to save.
>   He will take great delight in you,
> he will quiet you with his love,
>   he will rejoice over you with singing. (Zephaniah 3:17)

1. In this week's Prelude, what kind of anticipation do you see in Kathy's journal entries? For what kind of an earthly bridegroom is she praying?

_____

_____

2. Whether or not God brings a "Prince Charming" into our lives, we do have Someone who is much better than even our idea of Prince Charming. What are some of the truths you learn about Jesus from the following passages in John's Gospel?

    A. *In the beginning was the Word, and the Word was with God, and the Word was God. He was with God in the beginning. Through him all things were made; without him nothing was made that has been made.* (John 1:1–3)

    _____

    _____

    B. *In him was life, and that life was the light of men.* (John 1:4)

    _____

    C. *He was in the world, and though the world was made through him, the world did not recognize him.* (John 1:10)

    _____

3. Individuals, though they may not recognize Jesus, are often drawn to Him through His creation. The authors of *The Sacred Romance* believe that everyone has a sense

of this mystery through the music and beauty of the world. God says the same thing in His Word. Read Psalm 19:1–4.

A. According to the above psalm, how has God's voice gone out throughout the world?

_____

_____

B. How far-reaching is this language, according to the above psalm?

_____

_____

4. Do you remember any way that God called to you, through His creation, when you were young?

_____

_____

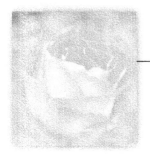

DAY 2

Because You Loved Me

When I (Kathy) was three, our family moved from Brooklyn to Long Island, which has some lovely wooded areas. I remember running around with my cousins on summer nights beneath a midnight blue-black sky. I'd be perspiring and then suddenly feel the cool tinge of the New York night on my face. (I can almost smell the air as I write this to you.) I'd lift my eyes to the stars in the clear sky and think, just for a moment, *There's Someone bigger than me out there.*

I was so taken with the moon and the stars, I dreamed of being the first female astronaut. I talked about it so much that my mother sent away for an astronaut suit. I thought it was the coolest. It was silver and had a helmet that opened. I dreamed about what it would be like to fly up there—and I wondered just how far the universe went. God was wooing me, as a little girl, through the wonder of the heavens.

When we realize that the God who made this amazing universe is also *mindful* of us, we are overwhelmed. Both David, the shepherd boy, and generations later, Mary, the mother of Jesus, expressed their wonder that such an amazing God was also personal:

David wrote:

When I consider your heavens,
 the work of your fingers,
the moon and the stars,
 which you have set in place,
what is man that you are mindful of him . . . ? (Psalm 8:3–4a)

Mary said:

My soul glorifies the Lord
 and my spirit rejoices in God my Savior,
for he has been mindful
 of the humble state of his servant (Luke 1:46–48)

Each believer has a different story to tell on how she made the transition from simply being aware that there *had* to be a God, to realizing that God was very personal, that He was mindful of her. He died for her, because He was not willing that she should perish, but wanted to be her Savior and the Love of her life.

I (Dee) had believed there was a God. And though I thought I was a Christian, it wasn't until I was a young wife and mother that I truly understood the claims of Jesus. I knew He had died on the cross—but I hadn't understood that it was for *me,* that He had taken the punishment for *my* sins. I also had not, until the Scriptures were opened to me, understood the holiness of God and my great need for deliverance. I remember wondering what Jesus would ask of me if I gave my life to Him. My sister quoted Matthew to me:

> *For whoever wants to save his life will lose it, but whoever loses his life*
> *for me will find it. What good will it be for a man if he gains the whole*
> *world, yet forfeits his soul? Or what can a man give in exchange for his*
> *soul?* (Matthew 16:25–26)

The words of Scripture, the very words of Jesus, began to teach my heart to fear:

> *Do not be afraid of those who kill the body but cannot kill the soul.*
> *Rather, be afraid of the One who can destroy both soul and body in hell.*
> (Matthew 10:28)

It was the fear of the Lord that brought me to my knees in repentance in our Indianapolis bedroom—and all that I really expected to happen was to be delivered of my fear of hell. That *did* happen, but so much more happened as well. His Spirit simply overwhelmed me. C. S. Lewis said he was "surprised by joy" at his conversion. Likewise, I could hardly believe that the God who made the universe was mindful of me, but it was clear that He was. "Heaven came down," as the old hymn joyously declares, "and glory filled my soul." He changed my perspective, put joy in my heart, and answered my infant prayers as quickly as a mother lifts her wailing newborn from her crib. Like a smitten schoolgirl, I walked on cloud nine for the next few months, wanting to tell everyone I met about Jesus.

It was not unlike the time in my life when I was falling in love with my husband. I remember how I would wake up each morning with a glow, trying to remember why I felt so full of anticipation: *Something wonderful is happening in my life—what is it? Oh yes, Steve!* I then leapt out of bed enthusiastically and dressed with special care, counting the moments until I would see his face and hear his wonderful masculine voice. Life was sweet, and everybody and everything was colored in the lovely hues of our budding love.

Now, in my first love time with Jesus, I would awake each morning with a glow, trying to remember why I felt so full of anticipation: *Something wonderful is happening in my life—what is it? Oh yes, Jesus!* I leapt out of bed, eager to be with Him, to see what He would whisper to me from His Word. Life was sweet, and everybody and everything was colored with the love we had for each other.

My (Kathy's) "once upon a time" began on August 5, 1978, when I prayed that Jesus would come and live inside my heart. The fact that this God whom I'd seen every Sunday hanging on the cross could be known intimately overwhelmed me. This was all such a revelation to me.

Walking out of church that day, I knew I had an escort. I felt like a beautiful bride, a princess. The perfect man had found me. Men had disappointed me so much, and all of a sudden I was face to face with perfect love and promises that wouldn't be broken. I knew in my spirit that His hand would never let go of mine, and that He had just been waiting for my "Yes." Just as in Dee's story, I woke up each morning trying to remember why I felt so full of anticipation.

For some believers, the transition is not so dramatic. You may have grown up hearing the story of Jesus, and you may not be able to remember the exact time that you put your trust in Christ. That is like someone who travels from Nebraska to Colorado and may not know exactly when she crosses the border. There comes a time when she *knows* she is in Colorado: There are signs saying "Denver—10 miles," there are snow-capped mountains, and there is a difference in the air.

In the same way, there are clear signs when a person has come into a personal relationship with Jesus Christ. If conversation about a deep love relationship with Jesus seems foreign to you, it is possible that you do *not* have what the Scripture calls saving faith, the kind of faith that makes you a child of God, that leads you out of the storm of the wrath of God into His perfect peace. Today you will study the signs of saving faith, which are based on a passage that the great preacher Charles Spurgeon called one of those bright stars that lead the sailor to the Port of Peace.[4]

Prepare your heart by continuing to memorize your verse.
Read Romans 10:9–10 carefully.

5. What are we to confess with our mouth? What does this statement mean?

_____

_____

6. The "heart," according to Scripture, does not mean the physical organ, but the source, or spring of motives; the seat of the passions.[5] The heart involves all of one's innermost being: her mind, her emotions, her will, the core of her life. How can you see, from Romans 10:9, that faith is not just intellectual assent to the facts?

_____

_____

In *The Divine Conspiracy*, Dallas Willard makes an analogy that anyone who has shopped at a supermarket and had her groceries scanned can understand. There is a "bar code," a little label on a can of beans that tells the scanner that this *is* a can of beans, along with the price. Some people believe that is how saving faith works. All you need to do (or have your child do) is repeat a certain prayer, acknowledge a certain creed, and the Divine Scanner beeps, saying you have made it into heaven.[6] But saving faith involves much more than just repeating a creed; it involves one's entire heart, will, and mind.

7. According to James 2:19, how do the demons exemplify those who give mental assent to the facts but do not have saving faith?

_____

_____

8. How does Ezekiel 36:26–27 describe a heart that has saving faith? How does this work?

_____

_____

9. How does Romans 10:10a bring up the issue of the "heart" again?

_____

10. What else, according to Romans 10:10b, is a sign of saving faith?

_____

11. Whether you received Jesus as a child or as an adult, there will be recognizable signs in your life if you have saving faith. According to Scripture, you should see the

If you have true saving faith, Jesus becomes a treasure chest of holy joy.[7]

—John Piper

following signposts. Ask yourself, "Have I seen each of the following in my life?" If you can remember any details about how it happened or how you felt, write them down— for it will help rekindle your gratitude.

A. Conviction: Truth comes with power and you are disturbed. (Acts 2:37)

_____

_____

_____

B. Repentance: You have a change of mind in regard to sin. (Acts 20:21)

_____

_____

C. Fear: Grace teaches your heart to fear a holy God. (Acts 2:37)

_____

_____

D. Desire for deliverance: You ask, what shall I do? (Acts 2:37)

_____

_____

E. Faith: You believe the promises are true and embrace them personally. (Romans 10:9)

_____

_____

F. Consciousness of peace and trust: His Spirit bears witness with your spirit, delivering you of fear. (Romans 8:15)

_____

_____

G. Thankfulness and praise: You are overwhelmed with gratitude, a gratitude that deepens as you grow.[8] (Acts 3:19 and 1 Corinthians 15:57)

_____

_____

If you *do not* see these signs in your life, if you *do not* have passion in your heart, and you are feeling conviction, you can be very thankful that His Spirit is working in you, teaching your heart to fear. Recognize your great need, recognize what Jesus did for you, and embrace Him with your whole heart. Call upon the name of the Lord and you *will* be saved (Romans 10:13). If you have further questions about this or would like someone to pray with you, ask your leader.

DAY 3

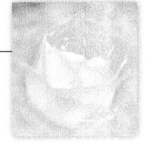

Beauty and the Beast

The sun was sinking behind the bare branches on the Nebraska prairie, transforming the bleak winter sky into a palette of lavenders and crimsons. Kathy and I lingered at the round oak table, steaming mugs of coffee in our hands, and talked about our favorite romantic books and movies and how they might be parables for falling in love with Jesus.

"My absolute favorite is *Beauty and the Beast*," Kathy said.

"You've said that before—but I don't get it. How does that relate to Jesus?"

"I never expected to love Jesus the way I do," she whispered, simply.

"Ohhhhh," I sighed, suddenly seeing the wonderful parallel. Swiftly, pictures began to come into my head. How at first Belle was repulsed by the beast, then drawn to him, and then, overcome with love for him. "Yes!" I nodded enthusiastically. "That's perfect, Kath. Though Jesus never repulsed me, I was certainly apathetic, then afraid, and then! I never, ever expected I would love Jesus the way I do today."

Kathy smiled, pleased. "I'm glad I'm finally getting you excited, Dee."

We laughed. The fiery Italian river had stirred up the quiet Scottish loch. "Tell me more," I urged.

"A few years ago when I was Christmas shopping," Kathy reminisced, "I came upon this wonderful porcelain figure of Belle dancing with the beast—looking just like they did in the movie. She was tiny, wearing that beautiful golden dress. He was huge, wearing that striking electric blue jacket. Her small white hand was engulfed in his paw. She was looking up at him, enraptured, and he was looking down at her with such adoration. Even though the figurine was expensive, I had to have it. I bought it for myself and put it in my curio. There's a little light shining down from above, illuminating the pair. When I look at them I am reminded that, every day, Belle lives inside me: the girl who wants to be pursued, sought after, swept up, and rescued."

We found ourselves smiling at each other as we pondered how great it is to feel that way. Especially as women.

We talked about other fairy tales and how they could be parables for falling in love with Jesus. *Snow White*, *Cinderella*, and *Sleeping Beauty* all have a prince who rescues the princess. Each "princess" was in great distress because of the forces of evil, yet each had a good and noble prince who sought her, swept her up, and rescued her.

Does this have *anything* to do with reality?

Yes. We have a Prince who is real. When we were in distress, in need of a deliverer, He sacrificed His life to rescue us. And He continues to rescue us. I (Kathy) know I am a miracle. I have been rescued from a hundred prisons. He rescued me from bulimia, from depression, from darkness in my soul. I am a work in process and I know I have a real-life Prince. And I (Dee) have been rescued from hell, from a meaningless life, from being the kind of wife who was destroying her husband and her marriage, and from countless other sorrows. I, too, am still being rescued, but as I've learned to submit to the Lord, as I've learned to trust, I have seen Jesus come through again and again.

We have seen our Prince do amazing things. As the psalmist said:

> I sought the LORD, and he answered me;
>   he delivered me from all my fears.
> Those who look to him are radiant;
>   their faces are never covered with shame.
> This poor man called, and the LORD heard him;
>   he saved him out of all his troubles.
> The angel of the LORD encamps
> around those who fear him,
>   and he delivers them.
> Taste and see that the LORD is good;
>   blessed is the man who takes refuge in him. (Psalm 34:4–8)

We have tasted and seen that He is good, and we desire to know Him better.

In our lives, God has provided each of us with mentors, women of depth who have trusted Him in significant ways and have experienced His power. We also have individuals of depth in His Word, mentors who can show us how to go higher with Jesus. Today we will consider Elizabeth and Zechariah. Each of these individuals trusted the Lord in significant ways and experienced His power, His deliverance, and His love. It is also important to realize that "rescue" does not always look the way we might think it will, but it is rescue nevertheless. Elizabeth and Zechariah's story demonstrates this beautifully.

Before you begin your lesson, you might sing or meditate on some love songs to Jesus (see Appendix A). Review your memory verse. Are you beginning to feel like a bride? A prayer that God will honor is a prayer to fall more in love with Jesus, and to grow in your confidence of His love for you.

Read Luke 1:5–7.

12. How does Luke describe Elizabeth and Zechariah in verse 6?

_____

_____

Blameless does not mean sinless. In Scripture, *blameless* means that the person is above reproach, cannot be accused, because she is endeavoring to walk in the light. It *does not* mean perfection, nor that she never steps out of the light, because we all do. But it *does* mean that as soon as she is aware that she has stepped out of the light she confesses, repents, and gets back in the light. There is a radiance in her life, a radiance that reflects the light of Christ.

13. Consider the concept of being blameless according to the following:

A. Read Philippians 2:14–16 and describe a "blameless" person.

_____

_____

B. Describe the life of a "blameless" person according to 1 John 1:7–9.

_____

_____

Make it your goal today to be "blameless." Walk in the light. If you get out, confess it immediately, turn from your sin, and get back in the light. You will know the joy of His presence.

14. Read Luke 1:7.

A. What sorrow permeated the lives of Elizabeth and Zechariah?

_____

B. Try to imagine Elizabeth as a young woman, living in a culture that tied a woman's worth to childbearing. Describe what feelings she might have had about herself and about her God.

_____

_____

C. We know, from Gabriel's words in Luke 1:13, that at least when they were younger, Elizabeth and Zechariah had prayed for a child. But the years passed and it didn't happen. Elizabeth probably went through menopause. Is there a desire of your heart that you have lifted before the Lord repeatedly—but He seems silent? If so, what is it? What do you know about God that could keep you from losing hope?

_____

_____

As the story continues, you will see that Elizabeth and Zechariah were eventually "rescued" from their barrenness. But it is important to remember the long years when their arms were empty and the pain and shame they endured. Joni Eareckson Tada, who has spent most of her life in a wheelchair, understands that though God can rescue with a miracle, often rescue looks different than we think it will:

> The core of God's plan is to rescue us from our sin. Our pain, poverty, and broken hearts are not his ultimate focus. He cares about them, but God cares most—not about making us comfortable—but about teaching us to hate our sins, grow up spiritually, and love him.[9]

Important things transpired in the lives of Elizabeth and Zechariah during those long years of waiting that could not have happened in any other way. Elizabeth learned to trust God when He wasn't making sense. Through this, she was equipped to become the mentor of Mary. Zechariah was disciplined for his lack of faith. Through this he learned to trust God more, discovering firsthand that all things are possible with God. As you study this story, consider not just their rescue from barrenness, but these other kinds of "rescues."

15. Read Luke 1:8–25.

A. Who appeared to Zechariah and what did he tell him?

_____

_____

B. Describe Zechariah's doubt and the discipline that followed. How might the discipline you see in this passage have produced growth in Zechariah? (Luke 1:18–22)

_____

_____

C. Zechariah responded remarkably to God's discipline. Find evidence of his growth in the song he sang after his son, John the Baptist, was born. (Luke 1:67–79)

_____

_____

16. Can you think of a time when God "rescued" you through discipline? Think of a time when you suffered consequences because of sin, or missed a blessing because you didn't trust Him—but you learned, and changed, and grew stronger.

_____

_____

Mary, Did You Know?

How much did Mary actually understand? To be chosen to be the mother of the Messiah was every Jewish maiden's dream. Mary's response of faith is significant:

> *"I belong to the Lord, body and soul," replied Mary. "Let it happen as you say."* (Luke 1:38a PHILLIPS)

But did Mary have any idea how hard her life would be? How could she have glimpsed the dark waters ahead? I (Dee) remember how apprehensive I was giving birth to my firstborn—yet I was surrounded by skilled nurses, doctors, and even a husband who was a medical student. Mary was going to give birth to *her* firstborn without even a midwife's help. And did Mary have any premonition her son would be so hated? When He was just a toddler, she had to flee in the night for Egypt. Can you even imagine? And did she know that one day she would watch His agony on the cross?

We doubt she ever imagined any of this. But God knew it all and cared so deeply. He prepared her for the dark waters ahead. He gave Mary a strong hint to go see Elizabeth. Three months with a woman like Elizabeth, a woman who had passed through the dark waters triumphantly, was exactly what His Princess needed.

Though you may have read this passage (Luke 1:26–40) many times, especially at Christmas, we want you to look at it with fresh eyes, to see how deeply God cared for each of these women, and met their needs. We pray you will realize that the same is true for you.

None of us knows what the future holds. But God wants us to put our hand in His and walk around the corner. That's what we see in Mary's life.

The Annunciation
BY CAVALIER D'ARPINO (1606)[ii]

∽

This remarkable event has been painted by many of the masters, each with their own interpretation. Gabriel is the angel of good news. He carries a lilly, the symbol of peace.

17. Read Luke 1:26–40.

    A. How does Luke date the time that Gabriel goes to see Mary? How does this begin to tie these two women together?

    _____

    _____

    B. Contrast Mary's response to Gabriel with Zechariah's response to Gabriel.

    _____

    _____

    C. How does Mary demonstrate a willingness to put her hand in the Lord's—even though she doesn't know exactly what is around the corner?

    _____

    _____

    D. List as many reasons as you can think of for Gabriel telling Mary about Elizabeth.

    _____

    _____

E. How does Mary's action described in verse 39 show a sensitivity to the leading of the Spirit?

_____

_____

R. ANNING BELL (1863–1933)[iii]

∽

This artist has portrayed Elizabeth's awe and humility bowing her knee to Mary in their greeting scene. There was such tenderness between these two women.

18. Read Luke 1:41–45.

A. According to verse 41, how did God equip Elizabeth to encourage Mary?

_____

_____

B. Mary had not told Elizabeth that she was pregnant. How do you think Elizabeth's words in verse 42 impacted her?

_____

_____

C. What emotions do you see in verse 43? Why do you think Elizabeth was so excited and honored by Mary's visit?

_____

_____

D. The excitement escalates with another supernatural happening. What is it, according to verse 44?

_____

_____

E. How does Elizabeth encourage Mary in her faith in verse 45?

_____

_____

F. How can you see God's care for Mary through this prophecy through Elizabeth?

_____

_____

Now it is Mary's turn to sing, and sing she does:

> *I'm bursting with God-news;*
>   *I'm dancing the song of my Savior God.*
> *God took one good look at me, and look what happened—*
>   *I'm the most fortunate woman on earth!*
> *What God has done for me will never be forgotten,*
>   *the God whose very name is holy, set apart from all others.*
> *His mercy flows in wave after wave*
>   *on those who are in awe before him.* (Luke 1:46–50 MSG)

Mary is dancing to the song of her Savior God, and so can we. The euphoria these women feel is the euphoria of women who have fallen deeply in love with the Lord, and they know, because they have passed through the stormy waters triumphantly, that their love is going to last. *His* love is going to last. They have reached the land of invincible love—not a land that is free of trouble, but a land full of confidence and joy.

19. We are told that Mary stayed with Elizabeth for three months. What are some ways you imagine Elizabeth might have mentored Mary for the difficult road ahead during those three months?

_____

_____

R. Anning Bell (1863–1933)[iv]

༄

This scene of domestic tranquility represents one artist's image of what transpired during those three months. We suspect that there were many deep times of sharing and prayer. What wisdom must have come from Elizabeth to strengthen and prepare Mary for the road ahead.

Day 5

Come Rain or Come Shine

Sometimes our Lord comes with a miracle, as He did for Elizabeth and Mary. Sometimes He simply gives us the grace to face the difficulties of life. I (Kathy) remember when my mother was hospitalized with cancer. Jesus got to me. It wasn't with a miracle, but He made His presence known. I tell the story in my book *My Life Is in Your Hands*.

"Kathy," the doctor began, soberly, "there wasn't just *one* tumor. There are multiple cancerous tumors throughout your mother's liver." I held on, still wanting a word of hope. But then he crushed that hope, saying, "I'm sorry. There's not much we can do."

"What does this mean?"

"Six months to two years," he answered.

I felt faint as so many emotions found their way through every part of my body. I thought about my dad, who died of colon cancer at forty-six years old. I thought about my mom's suffering. I thought about being orphaned.

I walked through the lobby toward a small chapel. No one was in the room, and I fell across one of the pews—facedown, on my stomach. The sound of my weeping filled the room. In my mind, I found myself looking out over a mountaintop. One side was full of a valley of voices rising in chorus: "What's the use? Haven't you had it?

Aren't you sick of all this cancer?" On the other side of the mountain was the reminder of all I'd known Jesus to be since 1978.

Then, to my surprise, His voice seemed to break through it all like lightning through a pitch-black sky:

"Am I not still God?"

"Am I not *still* God?"

I lay there motionless, and my breathing was quieted. I knew I could not leave that chapel and meet my mother after her surgery without responding to God's question. Deep inside, I knew that my answer would not only affect me but would also affect the last year of my mother's life. With swollen eyes and drenched face, I looked up to heaven and said, "Yes, Lord, You are still God."

Had I turned my back on God and left that question hanging in the air that day, I know that all I would have given my mother during the last year of her life would have been anger, bitterness, and fear.

My taking His hand in trust allowed me to walk alongside my mother and give her a supernatural comfort, peace, and hope. The exchange between us during that time will be forever etched on my heart. The whole dying process, ironically enough, was filled with Jesus' life. He met us at every turn—not without agonizing tears, questions, and long painful days, but He was there. During the final hours of my mother's life, I read Psalm 23 to her as she took deep breaths to recite it with me. She then led a room full of family and friends in the Lord's prayer.[10]

My Prince came through. And He will for you too. Always. Sometimes with a miracle, sometimes in another way. He surrounded me with a holy peace during my deepest sorrow—and He will for you as well.

You might want to prepare your heart by reviewing your memory verse.

20. How did God come through for Kathy during her mother's death?

    _____

    _____

21. Can you think of a time in your life when God didn't come through with a miracle, and yet, He did comfort you with His kisses: His presence, His prophecies, and His provisions? Share what you remember.

    _____

    _____

22. In each of the following, describe first the stressful situation Mary faced. Then find evidence that God came through for her in some way.

    A. Matthew 1:19–20

1) Stressful situation: _____

2) God's provision: _____

B. Matthew 2:16–19

1) Stressful situation: _____

2) God's provision: _____

C. Luke 2:25–35 and John 19:25–27

1) Stressful situation: _____

2) God's provision: _____

23. Meditate on your memory verse, Zephaniah 3:17.

A. What promises do you find in this verse?

_____

_____

B. How did you see the Lord "quieting" both Elizabeth and Mary with His love?

_____

_____

C. Do you have a stressful situation, or an area that has made you anxious so that you need to have the Lord "quiet you with His love"? What have you learned about God in this lesson that will help you to trust Him?

_____

_____

_____

Finale

REVIEW

24. Each woman should share, if she chooses, one thing that God impressed on her heart from this study, one way she was "kissed by the King."

_____

PRAYER

Cluster in threes or fours. Each woman, if she is willing, should lift up, in prayer, the stressful situation she wrote about in question 23C. The other women can support her in sentence prayers. For example:

> *Marie:* O Lord, I'm stressed about my relationship with my teenage daughter. We are angry with each other so often.
>
> *Amy:* Please give Marie and her daughter love for each other, understanding for each other's perspectives.
>
> *Carol:* I agree, Lord.
>
> *Heather:* Please give them some sweet times together before next week. Quiet them with your love.
>
> *Amy:* Yes, Lord.
>
> Silence
>
> *Carol:* Lord, I'm stressed about my eating habits. I'm out of control.
>
> Etc.

Please remember:

- Do not feel selfish about bringing up personal needs. God tells us to ask for help.
- Keep confidences.
- Don't try to fix the other woman's problem; rather, pray for her.

Looking for Love in All the Wrong Places

Prelude

Wrapping her arms around her slender legs, Kathy put her head down, hesitating. Then she told me, "Part of me doesn't want to tell this story, because it's *still* painful and because I don't want this man to know how devastated I was. But another part of me, the deepest part of me, is learning to die to myself. I know there's a vital parallel here, about how the wrong paths can seem so alluring and how important it is to obey the Spirit's first prompting. I didn't at this particular time in my life. It was as if I buckled myself into a roller coaster expecting to feel exhilarated, and all the while the car was not quite on the track. It led to destruction. I deceived myself, saying the cost couldn't be that high when, in reality, the cost was *heartbreakingly enormous.*"

So, here it is, from Kathy's heart:

Ellie and I were just becoming friends. She was telling me about a guy she had dated in college for a while.

I said, "Ellie, don't pawn off any of your 'exes' on me."

We laughed.

Ellie said, "But he's Italian."

I smiled. "Probably a *My Cousin Vinny* type."

"No, not at all! He's a very classy guy."

"Where is he spiritually?"

"He was close to the Lord once, and he led a campus Bible study, but he's fallen away."

That should have been it. But I left the door open a crack.

Ellie and her husband, Frank, had maintained a friendship with him, and he'd call and even visit sometimes. Once when I was at Ellie's, he phoned, and she said his name pointedly and gave me a look that communicated, *Do you want to talk to him?*

I nodded, smiling. *This could be fun,* I thought. I was like a little kid playing with matches.

I liked the sound of his voice, his demeanor. He made me laugh so easily. There was definitely chemistry. He made me feel so good. I wanted to talk to him more. There was a struggle going on in me, because I knew he wasn't close to God, but I thought surely there still had to be a little sensitivity to the Lord in him. I told myself, *What could it hurt just to meet him?* I knew deep down it wouldn't be a smart move. But I hushed that still, small voice.

Then, when I finally met him, I was quite overwhelmed because he was *so* good-looking. He dressed well, had his own business, and was a great conversationalist. It all awakened something in me. I felt more alive somehow.

It was a particularly vulnerable time in my life because my mother was dying, and my emotions were so raw. One night I came back home from visiting Mom in the hospital. I pulled into my driveway, not doing too well, and there he was, sitting on the steps to the house, waiting for me, looking like Prince Charming.

I was so smitten.

We were involved for a long saga of two and a half years, much of it by phone because I was on tour. I was a little bit more of the pursuer verbally, and even physically, and now I realize how wrong that was. He wasn't showing evidence of really having God in his life, and for me God was my whole life. On top of all of this, I knew deep down he didn't truly love me. He even said to me, "Troccoli, you're bigger than life. You're too much for me. I don't want to work that hard. With you I'll have a life of challenge, and I don't want it."

Even when the writing was on the wall, I refused to see it. One time I called him at home and he had another woman at his place. I was determined to fly out there and give him an ultimatum, tell him he had to choose her or me. I remember Ellie showing up at my door. She was so concerned about me. She said, "He doesn't love you, Kathy. *He does not love you.* What are you doing?"

How could I be so dumb as to not see that the choice had already been made? But sometimes you just can't see a situation clearly when you are in the midst of it. I remember feeling helpless. A war was going on in my soul. I think I knew he didn't love me, but there was a part of me that could not fathom that as much as I felt for him, he did not feel the same way back. It reminds me of the Bonnie Raitt song "I Can't Make You Love Me." There's a line in it that says I'll close my eyes so I don't have to bear seeing the love that I know you don't feel for me.

I absolutely know now that his lack of love was God's protection, because he wasn't God's choice for me. He was not God's man. But that doesn't mean that the whole experience didn't cause enormous damage to how I felt about myself as a woman and about how attractive and desirable I could be. Yet God, as He always does, has used time and His truth to continue to heal the wounds deep in my heart.

We underestimate the damage that can be done by looking for love in all the wrong places. Our choices have consequences, and often they are severe. God in His mercy can heal and even restore, but, oh, how He longs for us not to choose those paths.

The Book of Ecclesiastes was written as a warning, a flashing red light to two groups of people:

1. To those who do not know the Lord and are trying with things "under the sun" to fill up those places only God can fill.

2. To those who *do* know the Lord but lose that "first-love" passion and then, like Solomon, try to find their way out of the wilderness. They look for love in places that will leave them lost, discouraged, and empty-handed.

WATCH VIDEO #3: LOOKING FOR LOVE IN ALL THE WRONG PLACES

Dee will be referring to the opening of Ecclesiastes and the opening of the Gospel of John.

OPTIONAL NOTE-TAKING SPACE

_____

_____

_____

_____

_____

_____

GROUP RESPONSE TO THE VIDEO

A. What are some ways Dee tried to fill up the emptiness in her life before Christ? Could you identify with any of this?
B. Many believers trust God with salvation and assume they are free. What did Kathy's illustration of Lazarus illustrate?
C. What stood out to you from the video? How might you apply it to your life?

DAY 1

Is That All There Is?

Singer Peggy Lee was a diva from the sixties. Her song "Is That All There Is?" was a modern version of Ecclesiastes.[1] The theme of Ecclesiastes is "Vanity, vanity, all is vanity." The word *vain* or *vanity* means "something passing swiftly away." Like cotton candy, it tastes good for a moment, but then it quickly disappears and we are left with the taste of grit in our mouths. Life under the sun is sweet, and we are to enjoy

God's gifts of beauty, food, and sex—but none of them was ever meant to be abused. None of them was ever meant to meet our deepest needs. Philip Yancey writes:

> Ecclesiastes endures as a work of great literature and a book of great truth because it presents both sides of life on this planet: the promise of pleasures so alluring that we may devote our lives to their pursuit, and then the haunting realization that these pleasures ultimately do not satisfy. God's tantalizing world is too big for us. Made for another home, made for eternity, we finally realize that nothing this side of timeless Paradise will quiet the rumors of discontent.[2]

Trying to dull the ache in our hearts by running after things "under the sun," whatever those may be in your life—that is the "vanity of vanities." It is the opposite of the "Song of Songs," which is setting our affections on Jesus and finding the One, and the only One, who can give unfailing love.

Today you will get a preview of the haunting Book of Ecclesiastes.

Some songs that have particularly ministered to me (Dee) in preparing my heart for my time with God are "Holy, You Are Still Holy" and "Jesus, Name above All Names." You might want to sing these or others in Appendix A.

Review your memory verses from Week 1 and Week 2.

> As a bridegroom rejoices over his bride,
>   so will your God rejoice over you. (Isaiah 62:5b)

> The LORD your God is with you,
>   he is mighty to save.
> He will take great delight in you,
>   he will quiet you with his love,
>   he will rejoice over you with singing. (Zephaniah 3:17)

1. In this week's Prelude, Kathy tells a story about the devastation that occurred because of a path she chose to walk down. As you consider her story, how did she deceive herself?

   _____

   _____

2. Each day, we have choices, choices that involve staying in the light or wandering into the darkness. List a few ways you will be faced with those choices today. Then, next to that choice, write what the deepest part of you, the part that is the Bride of Christ, knows to be true that will help you choose to stay in the light.

   _____

   _____

3. Read Ecclesiastes 1:1–3.

 A. According to verse 1, who is the author?

 _____

 B. The theme of the book is stated the first time in the second verse. What is it and how would you describe the emotion?

 _____

 _____

 C. The word translated "vanity" or "meaningless" means "something passing swiftly away." What do you learn about these things according to the following passages?

 Proverbs 31:30 _____

 _____

 Matthew 6:19–21 _____

 _____

 D. What question is asked in Ecclesiastes 1:3?

 _____

 _____

 E. The "under-the-sun" perspective is the primary perspective of Ecclesiastes. It is the narrow view of life, the view that sees only what is visible. Contrast this view with the view described in Colossians 3:1–3.

 _____

 _____

When Gail Sheehy interviewed people for her book *Passages*, she found that in each stage of their lives, often with increasing desperation, people were hurrying "to pursue their own definition of a meaningful existence so that life would not become a repetition of trivial maintenance duties."[3]

Each time those with the narrow view try something "under the sun," they have hope, but then that hope turns to despair, for the visible things cannot possibly satisfy their deepest need. Only Jesus can do that.

4. Read Ecclesiastes 1:4–11.

 A. What word pictures does Solomon use in verses 5–7 to describe the monotonous cycle of life?

_____

_____

B. What are his conclusions, according to verses 8–11? What are his emotions?

_____

_____

Meditate on the key verse of the Book of Ecclesiastes:

> He has also set eternity in the hearts of men; yet they cannot fathom what
> God has done from beginning to end. (Ecclesiastes 3:11b)

5. What does it mean to have "eternity in your heart"?

_____

_____

6. What do we also learn about man from the above verse?

_____

_____

7. Why does Philip Yancey say, in the quote in today's introduction, that the Book of Ecclesiastes endures as a great book of truth?

_____

_____

8. If you were to maintain an eternal perspective today, how would it impact your choices? How do you think it might impact your emotions?

_____

_____

What Kind of Fool Am I?

Ecclesiastes was written, in part, as an evangelistic tract, a warning to the secular man or woman who is trying to find meaning "under the sun," apart from God and eternity. The author has done us the favor of rushing headlong into various pursuits "under the sun," only to find that, though they were exciting at first, he cannot shake the feeling that his life is not really accomplishing anything—that he is simply "chasing the wind."

But it is vital to realize that Ecclesiastes was not written primarily for unbelievers, but for *believers*. For the author, Solomon, had an intimate and sweet relationship with the Lord in his youth. God was pleased with Solomon and appeared to him twice. When Solomon was close to the Lord he gave us the sweetest song in the Bible, the "Song of Songs."

But though Solomon had it all, sometime in his middle years he grew careless. He ignored God's clear warning not to intermarry with women who worshipped other gods. God said to the Isrealites, "They will surely turn your hearts after their gods" (1 Kings 11:2b). But Solomon left the door open, and girls from all tribes and nations sauntered in. Solomon married seven hundred women and had three hundred concubines. They *did* turn his heart away, and Solomon lost so much. No longer did he have sweet fellowship with the Lord, or His anointing, or His power . . . all that was replaced with despair.

We scratch our heads, thinking, *Solomon! How could you have been so dense?* Solomon agreed. From his experiences he wrote the Book of Ecclesiastes to warn us of what will happen if we are not diligent in keeping our love relationship with the Lord alive.

Why, after Solomon had known the sweetness of fellowship with the Lord, did he go back to looking for love in all the wrong places? Why do any of us?

What I (Kathy) sense in myself and what I've sensed as I've talked to believers on the road is that we get impatient. We don't feel like there is enough immediate payback. We're lonely, we may be facing some kind of wilderness experience, and we don't want to wait for God to fill our needs. So we settle for a temporary filling. I have a friend who has recently left a homosexual lifestyle. She said, "I've got to tell you, I miss the high. I miss the camaraderie. I miss the titillation of it." My friend has stayed pure because she's hanging on to God and His promises, and she knows if she returns to her old life it is just going to be a quick fix with a false peace and then all will come crashing down. But it can be lonely waiting on God. It's like the Lazarus story. Jesus stayed where He was for two days, and Mary and Martha were thinking, *Are You there? Do You care?*

We are so easily deceived. It is like grabbing the tail of a snake. He will turn on us, overpowering us. If we try to restrain him and put him back in his box, he will refuse to be restrained. He is a "viper," Jonathan Edwards says, who hisses and spits at God.[4]

Solomon grabbed the tail of a snake and it turned on him, sinking its teeth into his tender flesh and poisoning what was one of the most promising lives in all of Scripture. A sadder but wiser man, Solomon wrote the Old Testament Book of Ecclesiastes as a warning to those who are tempted to look outside of God for love.

Prepare your heart by learning this week's memory verse:

Above all else, guard your heart,
for it is the wellspring of life. (Proverbs 4:23)

9. Read 1 Kings 3:4–15. Describe Solomon's sweet fellowship with the Lord in his youth.

_____

_____

10. Read 1 Kings 10:1–9. Describe Solomon's situation and the world's view of him.

_____

_____

EDWARD JOHN POYNTER (1836–1919)[v]

෨෯

The visit of the Queen of Sheba to King Solomon is portrayed by this artist with careful attention to scriptural detail. Note the columns, the throne, the twelve lions, the six steps (2 Chronicles 9:17–20). Solomon had everything the world values (wealth, fame, power, women), but it did not satisfy him. What our hearts are longing for cannot be found in this world.

⌒ *Falling in Love with Jesus Workbook*

11. Read 1 Kings 11:1–13.

    A. Why did God tell the Israelites not to marry the women from the surrounding nations? (vv. 1–2)

_____

_____

    B. Describe everything you can about Solomon's disobedience. (vv. 2–3)

_____

_____

    C. How is the heart of Solomon contrasted to the heart of his father, David? (vv. 4–6)

_____

_____

    D. What did Solomon do for Chemosh and Molech, two detestable gods? What do you think motivated him to do this? (vv. 7–8)

_____

_____

Chemosh and Molech demanded the sacrifice of children. The slain children were then placed in the gods' stone arms.[5] Chemosh was a god of the Moabites. (Next week we will be studying Ruth, who was a Moabite.)

    E. Find as many reasons as you can in verses 9–11 for God's heartbreak concerning Solomon.

_____

_____

    F. What was going to be the consequence of Solomon's attitude and behavior? How did God's love for David mitigate the consequence? (vv. 11–13)

_____

_____

Kings collected harems for status and for sexual pleasure. In the wisdom books of Proverbs and Ecclesiastes, Solomon expresses his great regret at his foolishness. (A fool, in Scripture, is one who fails to fear God.) Solomon, older and wiser, warns young men of the folly of pursuing sexual immorality.

12. Read Proverbs 5. List a few of the reasons Solomon warns each man to be satisfied with the "wife of his youth."

_____

_____

"Under the sun," sexual intimacy is the closest thing we have to worship. Since man cannot fathom that his deepest desire is for worship of God, he turns to sexual intimacy, even in the form of immorality. In *The Journey of Desire*, John Eldredge writes:

> Small wonder that many people experience sexual passion as their highest transcendence on earth. . . . For this exotic intimacy was given to us as a picture of something else, something truly out of this world. . . . To give yourself over to another, passionately and nakedly, to adore that person body, soul, and spirit—we know there is something special, even sacramental about sex. It requires trust and abandonment, guided by wholehearted devotion. What else can this be but worship? After all, God employs explicitly sexual language to describe faithfulness (and unfaithfulness) to Him. For us creatures of the flesh, sexual intimacy is the closest parallel we have to real worship. Even the world knows this. Why else would sexual intimacy become the number one rival to communion with God? The best imposters succeed because they are nearly indistinguishable from what they are trying to imitate. We worship sex because we don't know how to worship God.[6]

Are you tempted to walk down the path of sexual immorality to fill up the times of loneliness or boredom, or to ease the times of stress? Why do you think these paths seem alluring to you? How are you being deceived?

_____

_____

13. Read Ecclesiastes 2:1–11.

   A. As Solomon began to turn away from the Lord, what were some of the ways he tried to fill up the loneliness in his heart? (vv. 1–8)

_____

_____

_____

   B. Did Solomon find any pleasure in these "under-the-sun" pursuits? (v. 10)

_____

_____

C. How did he feel as time passed? (v. 11) Why, do you think?

_____

_____

The partying, the sizzle, the chemistry—it's all so attractive, but none of it is worth the sacrifice of God's peace. Is it fun? It can be. Does it give pleasure? Absolutely. But I don't know anyone, including myself (Kathy), who doesn't awaken after engaging in worldly pleasure to a feeling of emptiness, to the sad realization that the peace of God has slipped away. In the moment, it makes you feel alive. But it's that false aliveness, that false sense of passion, that false sense of euphoria.

Satan encourages us not to stop and think. He says, "Come on, it's great; don't miss it." We finally give in and say, "Okay . . ." And then, *boom!* He runs off and you're left with a pile of shame and guilt. You get close to the fire, then you enter the fire and find yourself trying to do the Flintstones back-pedal. I say it because I've lived it. I've crossed some lines. I've played with fire. I realize now it's all such death, and it breeds death. I want the peace of God more than anything. Sometimes in the peace of God you can feel a little lonely, but that's okay.

14. The Book of Ecclesiastes was written, in part, to warn us. Is there a way you could apply the warning to your life right now?

_____

_____

_____

Smoke Gets in Your Eyes

We underestimate the damage that can be done by looking for love in all the wrong places. Part of us thinks, *This is exciting, and maybe this will be it, and if it's not, at least I love the sound of it, the taste of it, the feel of it.*

Yet, when we play with fire, we get burned. Solomon asks:

Can fire be carried in the bosom without burning one's clothes? (Proverbs 6:27 NRS)

The smoke can be the greatest danger in a fire, even greater than the flame. It overcomes us, causing us to lose consciousness, or it blinds us, causing us to become disoriented, oftentimes leading to our death. Our senses become dulled. We wander about in the dark, making ungodly choices. The results can be sexual immorality, all kinds of addictions, and enslavement to our passions.

We can feel the burden in our conscience that something is wrong, but at the same time we convince ourselves that the consequences won't be that bad. How much poison has spilled out by breaking a confidence? How many lives have been destroyed by flirting with a married man? How much gluttony has been released by just one taste? We are amazed, when we look back, at the *tremendous cost* that was exacted from us. It almost doesn't seem fair, because the initial choices seemed so small and not all that risky. *No big deal*—or so we thought.

But perhaps the greatest cost to ourselves is that we miss the best. By grabbing the imposter, we have missed the real. Unbelievers miss God altogether; believers settle down in the lower places and miss the exaltation of going with Him to the mountaintops.

A study of the Book of Romans has often, historically, preceded revival. This book clearly shows us the great danger of ignoring God and going our own way. The passage we are studying today and tomorrow begins with an indictment against unbeliever and believer alike who have gone looking for love in all the wrong places. Paul says that every single person is responsible to seek God, for God has made His existence and character known through creation and through conscience. Everybody can see the power of God through His creation. And everybody has a still, small voice that whispers to his spirit, telling him what is right, and true, and good. The animals do not have this voice, but man, who has been given a soul, does. C. S. Lewis comments on this in the opening to his classic, *Mere Christianity:*

> Every one has heard people quarrelling. . . . we can learn something important from listening to the kinds of things they say. They say things like this: "How'd you like it if anyone did the same to you?"—"That's my seat, I was there first"—"Leave him alone, he isn't doing you any harm"—"Why should you shove in first?"—"Give me a bit of your orange, I gave you a bit of mine." . . .

> Now what interests me about all these remarks is that the man . . . is appealing to some kind of standard of behaviour which he expects the other man to know about. And the other man very seldom replies: "To hell with your standard." Nearly always he tries to make out that what he has been doing does not really go against the standard, or that if it does there is some special excuse. . . . It looks, in fact, very much as if both parties had in mind some kind of Law or Rule of fair play or decent behaviour or morality or whatever you like to call it, about which they really agreed.[7]

Paul says the same thing, noting that even the Gentiles, who did not have the law of God, "show that the requirements of the law are written on their hearts, their consciences also bearing witness" (Romans 2:15).

As you read of God's wrath against mankind today, note that the reason man has gone looking for love in all the wrong places is *not* because of ignorance, but because he has chosen to ignore God.

Review your memory verse.

15. From today's introduction, answer the following questions:

    A. What question does Solomon ask in Proverbs 6:27?

    _____

    _____

    B. Why can the smoke be a greater danger than the flame in a fire? What is the application for us?

    _____

    _____

    C. Every person, the Book of Romans says, is responsible to seek God, for God's power and divine nature have been revealed (even apart from His Word) to everyone. How has God done this both outwardly and inwardly?

    _____

    _____

16. Read Romans 1:18–23.

    A. From the introductory statement of Romans 1:18, list everything you can discover about the recipients of God's wrath.

    _____

    _____

    B. What qualities of God should be obvious to every individual, and why? (Romans 1:19–20 and 2:15)

    _____

    _____

Man's primary problem is not an intellectual problem, but a heart problem. God reveals enough of Himself, through creation and through man's conscience, that man should be stirred to seek Him. James D. G. Dunn, in the *Word Biblical Commentary,* explains that, according to the above, "man is recognized as a responsible agent in face of this revelation, so that his failure to respond appropriately is not simply a lack of perception, a defect in spiritual capacity, but a moral failure, a culpable act, 'without excuse.'"[8]

C. According to Romans 1:21, what did people fail to do that led to the darkening of their hearts?

_____

_____

D. What did this failure to seek God and to be filled with thanks toward Him lead to, according to Romans 1:22–23?

_____

_____

E. Though this passage is directed primarily to pagans, it is also relevant to the Jews, for the example Paul gives in the above passage is that of God's people. Read a fuller description of this account in Psalm 106:19–22. What did they forget? What did they do?

_____

_____

We shake our heads in amazement at the Israelites, who built and worshipped a gold idol right after God had parted the Red Sea and led them through. Why couldn't they trust Him? Why couldn't they wait for Moses to come down from the mountain? Couldn't they see how foolish they were being? Yet we do the same thing. When God does not immediately deliver us, we may drive, in a kind of panic, to the mall, hoping a new outfit will deliver us from the boredom; or we may open the freezer door and down the Rocky Road, hoping to ease the stress; or we may run to the familiar arms of a secret sin, the adulterous lover we thought we had left behind, thinking that secret sin will fill the chasm of loneliness in our heart. But, like the Israelites, instead of finding deliverance, we find ourselves returning to slavery, to emptiness, and to futility. Smoke gets in our eyes. We deceive ourselves, becoming content with assurances of salvation. We can no longer see our Lover or hear His cry to "come higher."

F. When you are stressed, lonely, or bored, what is your comfort?

_____

_____

To Love You More

We don't think of ourselves as idolators, but anytime we allow something or someone to be what only God should be to us, we are, indeed, idolators. Generally speaking, men often idolize the things that bring them status: fame, wealth, and power. Women may idolize those things as well, but often, as members of the relational sex, we idolize people. We may live our lives to please people rather than God. We may look to our friends, our husband, or our children for the security and peace that only God can give. We may even experience the bondage of excessive attachment, and bring pain to others through control, manipulation, and unreasonable demands. These are all symptoms of idolatry.

Idolatry is not God's heart for us. Corrie ten Boom, who lived out her faith in Nazi concentration camps, said that if we cling to someone or something too tightly, our loving Father will pry our fingers away.

How will He pry our fingers away?

Often, He allows us to feel the consequences of idolatry. He does this not to be cruel, but because He wants what is best for us, He wants us to let go of our idols and worship Him. The good gifts He gives us of family, friends, careers, sex, food, etc.— all are meant to be enjoyed, but not to be worshipped. When we worship them, He will bring pain into our lives. Why? Because He loves us.

The particular example of sin that Paul gives in Romans 1 is the practice of homosexuality. It is interesting to see that the root sin of homosexuality, whether male or female, is idolatry. People worshipping people. But it is important for you to see that this pattern could apply to any sin. When we worship something or someone other than God, God will often "give us over," allowing us to feel the painful consequences of our misplaced worship. Anything other than God, even the sweetest object, is not worthy of worship, and sooner or later will reveal its feet of clay. The result? Great pain and heartache.

17. From today's introduction, answer the following questions:

   A. How would you define *idolatry?*

   _____

   _____

   B. Why does a good God allow us to feel the pain of idolatry?

   _____

   _____

C. If you are honest with yourself, what do you tend to idolize? Consider what you think about the most, what you couldn't live without, and where you run for comfort.

_____

_____

18. Read Romans 1:24–32.

A. In verse 24, you see the phrase "God gave them over," a phrase you will see repeated two more times in this chapter. It is a frightening judgment. In this case, to what does God give them over?

_____

_____

B. According to verse 25, what did they worship instead of God?

_____

_____

C. In verse 26, to what does God give them over? How is this a further step down?

_____

_____

D. What example of sin is given in verses 26–27? What do you learn about the pain of this sin?

_____

_____

Though the practice of homosexuality is the sin mentioned, other sins, particularly sins of the flesh, have the same power to inflame our lusts and put us into bondage. Gluttony, pornography, abuse of drugs or alcohol, etc.—all can enslave us and make our lives a living hell. Their grip is as strong as quicksand, and a person needs a helping hand to get out.

E. In verse 28, to what does God give them over?

_____

When you walk away from the light, your eyes begin to get accustomed to the darkness, and it doesn't seem so dark anymore. You become confused, disoriented. Soon what you are doing becomes natural and right in your eyes. Because you have not repented and returned to the light, you have been given over to a depraved mind.

F. Describe other general characteristics that result from turning away from the worship of God. (vv. 29–31)

_____

_____

G. What is the final step of depravity? (v. 32b)

_____

_____

Often, well-intentioned but misled individuals preach that we should not try to change the homosexual, the sexually promiscuous, the obese, and others who are in bondage because of abusing God's good gifts. They tell us that God is love, and that we are not being loving. We agree that God loves sinners (and as sinners ourselves, we are so thankful!) and that His children must love sinners as well. The Christian world *has* failed miserably in showing love, particularly to homosexuals. But love does not mean that we should condone hurtful and unholy behavior. When I (Kathy) wrote *Live for the Lord*, I wanted to tell people that my God is love, but He also is holy. We must encourage one another to turn from behavior that is hurtful to ourselves and others, and to embrace God's best. It is a lie of the enemy that says we cannot change. We don't have to be enslaved by anything. God clearly tells us that nothing is impossible with Him (Luke 1:37) and that He can set us free (John 8:32).

19. Is there a sin of the flesh that is particularly tempting to you? How have you felt the consequences of this sin in your body? How has this temptation, whatever it is, proved itself to be a false god, one that gives you a temporary lift but then leaves you desperate?

_____

_____

20. Paul has primarily been addressing the sin of the Gentiles, but now he is going to deflate the pride of the Jews as he turns the searching light of God toward them in Romans 2.

A. Who else has no excuse, and why? (Romans 2:1–3)

_____

B. How have those who are familiar with the law fallen short of it? (Romans 2:17–24)

_____

_____

21. What are some of the principles you know to be true, because of God's Word, yet struggle to obey?

_____

_____

Believer and unbeliever alike are in desperate need of God's grace. This is where Paul is headed in the Book of Romans. We are so depraved that we cannot, in our own effort, measure up to God's holy standard. We need His grace, we need His Spirit, and we need the faith to trust that if we die to ourselves, He will continue to deliver us from bondage.

DAY 5

To Dream the Impossible Dream

In *The Journey of Desire*, John Eldredge writes:

> This may come as a surprise to you: Christianity is not an invitation to become a moral person. It is not a program for getting us in line or reforming society. It has a powerful effect on our lives, but when transformation comes, it is always the *aftereffect* of something else, something at the level of our hearts. At its core, Christianity is an invitation to *desire*.[10]

When Jesus talked to the woman at the well, He did not talk to her about morality. He did not chastise her for looking for love in all the wrong places (five husbands and her current live-in boyfriend). Instead, He talked to her about her *desire*, about her *thirst*. He wanted her to look deep into her soul, into the eternity that God had set in her heart (see Ecclesiastes 3:11). He wanted her to come to Him and enter into a deep love relationship with Him—and He knew that then the rest would fall into place.

Ecclesiastes reveals the deep thirst that each of us has. In a sense, Ecclesiastes is the drumbeat preparing the way for Christ. All of the haunting questions of Ecclesiastes are answered in Christ. That light shines down on us the day we cry out for deliverance and receive Christ. A. W. Tozer writes:

> The moment the Spirit has quickened us to life in regeneration our whole being senses its kinship to God and leaps up in joyous recognition.[11]

That moment happened for me (Dee) in 1966. And it happened for me (Kathy) in 1978. Each of us vividly remembers how His Spirit testified with our spirit that we were forgiven, that we were God's children. Each of us had been plagued by questions, the same kind of questions that run through the Book of Ecclesiastes, but when we received Christ, we received answers. How? Through the miracle of His Spirit. God began us on a journey that day, a journey of setting us free. We had found God, yet we still had to pursue Him.

Prepare your heart in a way that is helpful to you. You might sing, or kneel, or meditate on your memory verse.

Come near to the holy men and women of the past and you will soon feel the heat of their desire after God."

—A.W. Tozer

22. From today's introduction, answer the following questions:

   A. How did Jesus approach the woman at the well? What was her deepest need? What were the symptoms she had that resulted from not recognizing her need?

   _____

   _____

   B. What does A. W. Tozer say we can learn from the holy men and women of the past?

   _____

   _____

23. In each of the following, state first the haunting question or lament of the man with blinders, as portrayed by Solomon in Ecclesiastes. Then explain, according to the New Testament Scripture reference, how light is shed on that blindness through Christ.

   A. *Is there anything of which one can say, "Look! This is something new"?* (Ecclesiastes 1:10)

   _____

   Therefore, if anyone is in Christ, he is a new creation; the old has gone, the new has come! (2 Corinthians 5:17)

   _____

   B. *So I hated life, because the work that is done under the sun was grievous to me. All of it is meaningless, a chasing after the wind. I hated all the things I had toiled for under the sun, because I must leave them to the one who comes after me. And who knows whether he will be a wise man or a fool? Yet he will have control over all the* work into which I have poured my effort and skill under the sun. This too is meaningless. So my heart began to despair over all my toilsome labor under the sun. (Ecclesiastes 2:17–20)

_____

"Do not store up for yourselves treasures on earth, where moth and rust destroy, and where thieves break in and steal. But store up for yourselves treasures in heaven, where moth and rust do not destroy, and where thieves do not break in and steal." (Matthew 6:19–20)

_____

C. Man's fate is like that of the animals; the same fate awaits them both: As one dies, so dies the other. All have the same breath; man has no advantage over the animal. (Ecclesiastes 3:19)

_____

"I am the resurrection and the life. He who believes in me will live, even though he dies; and whoever lives and believes in me will never die." (John 11:25)

_____

D. Again I looked and saw all the oppression that was taking place under the sun: I saw the tears of the oppressed—and they have no comforter; power was on the side of their oppressor— and they have no comforter. (Ecclesiastes 4:1)

_____

"Come to me, all you who are weary and burdened, and I will give you rest." (Matthew 11:28)

_____

E. As a man comes, so he departs, and what does he gain, since he toils for the wind? All his days he eats in darkness, with great frustration, affliction and anger. (Ecclesiastes 5:16–17)

_____

"I have come that they may have life, and have it to the full." (John 10:10b)

_____

Once we have come into a personal relationship with Christ, His light illuminates our darkness, His grace covers our sins, and His Spirit quickens us, giving us power to do what we could not do on our own. But it is vital that we see the new birth as the *beginning* of our journey, and continue to press hard after God, desiring to know Him better.

24. Moses and David were two who went to the higher places with God. What do you learn about each of their hearts from the following passages?

   A. Exodus 33:12–18 (Moses) _____

   _____

   _____

   B. Psalm 63:1 (David) _____

   _____

   _____

Finale

REVIEW:

25. Each woman should share, if she chooses, one way she was "kissed by the King."

   _____

   _____

PRAYER

   How vital it is that we pray for one another's hearts. So often we pray for transitory troubles and forget to pray for the most important thing: our hearts, our love relationship with Jesus. Today, cluster in threes and fours and pray through God's Word for each other. Follow this pattern, substituting the names of the women in your small group as you take turns lifting one another up to the throne of God.

   Kim: Father, please help Emily, above all else, to guard her heart, remembering it is the wellspring of life.

   Emily: Yes, Lord, please help me.

   Jo: Please help Emily to love You with all her heart, all her mind, all her strength, and all her soul.

   Pause

   Emily: O Lord, please help Jo, above all else, to guard her heart, all through the day, all through the week. Help her remember that everything flows from her heart.

   Etc.

ACT I

First Love

❦

Orchestra
allegro scherzando
(Begin briskly, keeping the tempo
lively and the spirit cheerful)

It Had to Be You

Prelude

I (Kathy) have been traveling for many years. My concerts and speaking engagements take me to places all over the world. Sometimes they are as dull as a row of fast-food restaurants in Nowhere, USA, but sometimes they are as exciting as dining at a fine restaurant with the best view of the sun setting over the Caribbean. It is in these lovely faraway places that the fire in me to share my life with someone still burns with a passionate flame:

> *January 19, 1996*
>
> French toast . . . coffee . . . On a balcony this morning—overlooking the ocean . . . Cancun, Mexico. I am overwhelmed by some of the amazing things I get to experience because God has given me a voice.
>
> Of course, as you know by now, there are never these kinds of moments when my thoughts don't turn to you.
>
> To share this with you someday: walking along the beach hand in hand, hearing the serenade of the waves, breathing in the fresh night air as the sun sets gently on the horizon—ah . . . the romance of it all . . .
>
> *January 29, 1995*
>
> It's my second night of the "Forever Friends" cruise. . . . It's absolutely lovely here.
>
> Every time I experience anything like this—I think about you—and yearn to be with you—I long to make memories with you.
>
> You're somewhere in the world tonight.
>
> I miss you.

When I (Dee) first read these entries, I was struck by the parallel of Kathy's yearning and the yearning that God has for each of us. He wants us to be so close to Him. Kathy told me, "It's such a sweet thought to think that God could be lonely for me."

It can seem difficult to believe that He really does yearn for us. He is so great, and we are so small. He is so holy, and we are so unholy. But just as we are relational, so is the One in whose image we are made. God doesn't need anything, but He does want our love and devotion. When did He begin to dream of a relationship with us?

> *Long before he laid down earth's foundations, he had us in mind, had*
> *settled on us as the focus of his love, to be made whole and holy by his love.*
> *Long, long ago he decided to adopt us into his family through Jesus Christ.*
> *(What pleasure he took in planning this!)* (Ephesians 1:4–5 MSG)

God is the pursuer. He is lonely for us. He is the Bridegroom longing for His Bride.

WATCH VIDEO #4: IT HAD TO BE YOU
Dee will be teaching from the Book of Ruth.

OPTIONAL NOTE-TAKING SPACE

_____

_____

_____

_____

GROUP RESPONSE TO THE VIDEO
A. Why was Ruth, as a Moabite, a surprising bride, a surprising daughter-in-law? What can you learn from this?
B. Why was Boaz a wonderful groom? What qualities did you see in him that made him an appropriate Christ figure?
C. How did Ruth abandon herself?
D. Why does Kathy believe spirituality is so popular today? Do you agree?
E. What stood out to you from the video, and why?

DAY 1

When I Fall in Love

In biblical times, and into the eleventh century, the Jewish marriage ceremony had two distinct parts. The first part of the ceremony was the betrothal, as in the betrothal of Mary and Joseph. This was called the *erusin* (meaning "forbidden"). After the betrothal, the woman was considered the man's bride. It was a permanent and legally binding commitment, though the marriage had not been consummated.

Before the second part of the ceremony, there was a period of separation. This was a time of preparation. The bride would work on her wedding gown and the bridegroom would add a room to his father's house for his new wife and himself.

Then, when the *bridegroom's father* felt all was ready, the bridegroom would come, in a great processional, for the bride. The bride didn't know when this would be—so she needed to always be ready. When he came, the second part of the ceremony was performed, a seven-day celebration culminating in a great wedding feast. This second part of the ceremony was called the *nissuin* (meaning "carrying" or "taking").[1] The bridegroom would then take his bride home.

This makes the picture Jesus paints particularly meaningful. We are betrothed to Him. We are His Bride. There is a ring on our finger. But we are in the period of separation. He is preparing a place for us. Jesus said:

> *In my Father's house are many rooms; if it were not so, I would have told you. I am going there to prepare a place for you. And if I go and prepare a place for you, I will come back and take you to be with me.* (John 14:2–3)

When Jesus comes, He will take us away, far above this world. Our finite minds cannot fathom the place He is preparing. But we do know we will live forever without shedding a tear, we do know we will have eternal peace, and we do know we will be reunited with brothers and sisters in Christ. But best of all, we will be with Jesus face to face.

To prepare your heart for today, begin learning the memory verses for this week. These beautiful words of Ruth, which have immortalized her, are used often in wedding ceremonies. However, as you learn them, think of yourself saying them to your ultimate Bridegroom, Jesus. Consider their meaning in that sense.

> *Entreat me not to leave thee, or to return from following after thee: for whither thou goest, I will go; and where thou lodgest, I will lodge: thy people shall be my people, and thy God my God:*
> *Where thou diest, will I die, and there will I be buried: the LORD do so to me, and more also, if ought but death part thee and me.* (Ruth 1:16–17 KJV)

1. How do the above words of Ruth reflect abandonment?

    _____

    _____

2. On a metaphorical level, if you, as the Bride of Christ, were to say the above words to Jesus, meaning them with your whole heart, what might it mean?

Consider where Jesus went, and what it would mean to die as He died, to be "crucified with Christ" (Galatians 2:20).

_____

_____

Privately pray through Ruth's words, asking the Spirit to help you understand their depth and to give you the desire for complete abandonment to Jesus. A song I (Dee) sometimes sing as a prayer before I study is "Open Our Eyes," substituting "my" for "our" (see Appendix A).

3. Referring to today's introduction, describe everything you can about the two parts of the Jewish wedding ceremony.

    _____

    _____

4. Read Matthew 1:18–19. Mary and Joseph have gone through the first part of the ceremony. What evidence can you find in this passage that the _erusin_, or first part of the Jewish ceremony, was regarded as more binding than the contemporary practice of engagement?

    _____

    _____

5. The first time Jesus came to earth it was to woo us and win us. If we have put our trust in Him, we have been through the first part of the ceremony. We are betrothed. What do you learn about this betrothal in Hosea 2:19–20?

    _____

    _____

6. Right now, we are in the period of separation. Jesus is coming back to wed us, but in the meantime, we are to be working on our wedding gowns. Read Revelation 19:6–9 and see if you can discern what it would mean, in a metaphorical sense, to prepare your wedding gown.

    _____

    _____

7. In the Jewish wedding ceremony, the bridegroom prepared a place for the bride during the period of separation. How does this relate to Jesus, according to John 14:1–4? Write down everything you discover.

    _____

    _____

When I (Kathy) was looking for songs for my *Sounds of Heaven* record, my manager, the record company, and I listened to a tape by Chris Rice. Chris's tape was simple, with just Chris and his guitar. The last song was called "Missing You." It didn't have a dramatic commercial-type chorus in which you recognize, *Wow, that's a hit song.* But, oh, how it touched me.

> I heard about the day You went away
> You said You had to go prepare a place
> And even though I've never seen Your face
> I'm missing You
> I lie awake tonight and watch the sky
> And I wish it didn't have to be so high
> 'Cause I'm belonging on the other side
> And I'm missing You

I put my head down as I listened to the lyrics. I found myself weeping. When the song was over, I looked up and realized I was the only one who had been touched so deeply. I think that's because a single person has a little more opportunity to have a longing and an ache for intimacy than does a person in a good marriage. I can't cuddle at night, nor can I have that sense of belonging when I turn out the lights that married people can. So, yes, I do miss Jesus. I long for Him to come and sweep me into His arms, far beyond this world.

8. If you are a single woman, do you think that your singleness has enhanced your relationship with Jesus? If so, share.

    _____

    _____

9. The apostle John had a vision of that great day when Christ will come back for His Bride. What did he hear and see, as described in Revelation 19:6–9?

    _____

    _____

When my (Dee's) daughter was married, the wedding ceremony was divided into three parts, based on the above, and inspired by the Song of Songs.

Part I. *In the Garden*
This part represented the courtship. Sally and Jeremie came out from the back of the flower-filled stage of the church, together with their friends (whom they called the daughters and sons of Jerusalem). Sally was wearing a blue silk dress, and

Jeremie was wearing a gray suit. Their friends asked them, in chorus, "How is your beloved better than others?" (Song of Songs 5:9a). Then they each shared how and why they had fallen in love with the other. Sally sang "Our Love Is Here to Stay" to Jeremie. Then they each explained why they had fallen in love with Jesus, sharing their testimonies. At the close of this part, Sally said to Jeremie: "Now you see me as your betrothed, but in a little while you will see me as your bride."

Part II. *The Period of Separation*
During this part Sally and Jeremie left and changed into their wedding clothing while Amy Shreve, a soloist and harpist, performed a mini-concert of songs based on the Song of Songs.

Part III. *The Joining of the Bride and Bridegroom*
This part was similar to a traditional wedding ceremony, although our pastor explained the symbolism behind many of our traditions. For example, the blowing of the trumpet before the bride appears is meant to remind us of that great and glorious day when the trump of God will sound and we, the Bride of Christ, will be caught up together with Him in the air.

10. If you were to answer the question, in regard to Jesus, "How is your beloved better than others, most beautiful of women?" (Song of Songs 5:9a), how would you answer?

_____

_____

> *God might have given Adam another man to be his friend, to walk and talk and argue with if that was his pleasure. But Adam needed more.*[2]
>
> —Elisabeth Elliot

DAY 2

My Girl

Eve, the first bride, was breathtakingly beautiful to Adam. When he saw her, he knew. She was his completion. Though both Adam and Eve were made in the image of God, they were different; they were male and female.

In *The Divine Romance*, Gene Edwards tells the story of the formation of the first bride (Eve) and the last bride (the Bride of Christ). Edwards notes some intriguing parallels:

- As Adam was lonely for Eve, God is lonely for us.
- As Adam was ecstatic when he saw Eve, God is looking forward, with great anticipation, to the completion of His holy Bride.
- As Eve reflected the nature of Adam, so the Bride of Christ is to reflect the nature of Christ.[3]

11. Read Genesis 2:18–25.

   A. What reasons does God give for creating a bride for Adam? (v. 18)

   _____

   _____

   B. What parallel can you see to the Bride of Christ?

   _____

   _____

   C. When and how did God create Eve? (v. 21)

   _____

   D. Describe Adam's enthusiasm and feelings when God presented Eve to him. (v. 23a)

   _____

   _____

Do you realize that Jesus has the same kind of love for you? Review your memory verses from weeks one and three. Write them out without looking at them. Make sure they are etched in your heart, for they will help you to have confidence in Christ's love for you.

_____

_____

—Isaiah 62:5b

_____

_____

—Zephaniah 3:17

He loves you. You are the object of His affection. You are in the period of separation, and as you learn to abandon yourself to Him, He is making you more and more beautiful. Jewish brides made elaborate wedding gowns during the time they were waiting for their bridegroom to return, desiring to be breathtaking when their groom arrived. *Our* wedding gowns are our characters: our purity and radiance, our integrity, and our growing devotion to Him. His Spirit helps us to prepare for the appearance of our Bridegroom. Charles Spurgeon puts it like this:

> As the form of Eve grew up in silence and secrecy under the fashioning hand of the Maker, so at this hour is the Bride being fashioned for the Lord Jesus.[5]

DAY 3

Haven't Got Time for the Pain

Perhaps one of the reasons weddings often move us to tears is because of the sheer beauty of commitment, of a man and a woman so in love that they are willing to stand before a holy God and promise to forsake all others and to cherish one another forever.

Yet we live in a time when fewer people are willing to pay the price of true love. Commitment is postponed, sometimes avoided altogether. It's fashionable today to simply move in together without the promise, without the blessing of God.

In the same way, "spirituality" is very fashionable right now. It's chic. It's cool to be spiritual. You can watch the Grammys, Emmys, or Oscars and hear people thank "God" all the time. But I (Kathy) often wonder, *What god are they thanking?* You can't turn a channel late at night without hearing the psychic network enticing naive callers. Some people rub stones, hang crystals, and light candles, believing they can possess or unleash certain powers. Why is all this "spirituality" so popular—and why are people so accepting of it? I believe it is because it requires nothing from you. Sacrifice is an unpopular concept in this country.

But Jesus Christ requires your life. He requires your heart, soul, and mind. He requires the cross. As in the parable Jesus told, people have all kinds of excuses as to why they refuse the invitation to the Wedding Banquet. The truth is, they are unwilling to die to themselves. *They don't understand that dying is the key to living, that with abandonment abundant life springs forth, that with abandonment comes a supernatural peace, a supernatural hope.*

Both Dee and I have had women come to us who are deeply concerned about what they'd have to give up if they followed Jesus. They ask questions like:

- Can I still sleep with my boyfriend?
- Can I still party on weekends?

- What if my husband rejects me, thinking I've become a religious fanatic?
- Will I have fun? Will I be happy?

Let's just address this last question right off the bat. "Happy" is not the goal. "Happy" is fleeting. "Happy" gives you thrilling roller-coaster rides. The goal is loving Jesus. Then, and only then, do you experience an inextinguishable joy. Jesus doesn't require things of us or ask things of us because He's a dictator who gets a kick out of being in control and making us miserable. He is Lord. He is God. The "rules" are because He knows what is best for us. As you grow and know Him more, your trust grows and you are truly able to see why He requires certain things of you. He always acts out of love. That doesn't mean you will not feel a loss, or that the process won't be painful. Sacrifice is frightening. The cross is excruciating. But as bleak and as dark and as hopeless as things may seem, they were as bleak to Christ's followers when He hung in agony dying on the cross, and there was a resurrection three days later. God had a perfect plan for Christ and He has a perfect plan and purpose for *your* life. We must remember that *with every cross we pick up, with every death, there will always be a resurrection.*

To prepare your heart for today's lesson on commitment, review your memory verses. Pray them, without looking at them, as a prayer to Jesus.

12. Why do you think spirituality is so popular today?

_____

_____

13. Read Luke 14:15–35.

A. What excuses are given for refusing to come to the great Wedding Banquet? (vv. 18–20)

_____

_____

Material concerns are dominant, but one man tries a more "sanctified" excuse, that of being newly married. But that is weak as well, for, as Darrell Bock explains,

> The Old Testament did free a newly married man from certain obligations like war (Deut. 20:7; 24:5), but it is hard to see how marriage would disqualify one from attending a social meal. . . . Such excuses are lame, even insulting, in the light of the occasion.[6]

B. What excuses do people give today for not responding to Christ's invitation?

_____

_____

C. In the parable, how does the master respond when he hears about the excuses? (v. 21)

_____

_____

D. What will happen to the people who refused the invitation? (v. 24)

_____

E. How does this parable make it clear that God's people will be found in surprising places?

_____

_____

Tomorrow we will be considering how God invited two "surprising" women to His banquet. Orpah and Ruth were Moabites. One of the primary gods worshiped in Moab was Chemosh, who demanded sexual immorality and the sacrifice of children. Generally speaking, the Jews despised the Moabites.

14. Read Luke 14:25–35.

A. What statement does Jesus make to the great crowds who are following Him? (v. 25)

_____

_____

Darrell Bock writes that the call to "hate" is not literal, but rhetorical. He explains:

> Otherwise, Jesus' command to love one's neighbor as oneself as a summation of what God desires makes no sense (Luke 10:25–37). The call to hate simply means to "love less" (Gen. 29:30–31; Deut. 21:15–17; Judg. 14:16). . . . Following Jesus is to be the disciple's "first love." This pursuit is to have priority over any family member and one's own life, which means that other concerns are to take second place to following Jesus.[8]

B. How can you know if you've crossed the line from loving your children, your husband, or your friends to worshipping them? What are some ways you can discern whether Jesus is your "first love" or not?

_____

_____

_____

C. What do you think it means to carry your cross and follow Jesus? (See also Luke 9:23–24 and Galatians 2:20.)

_____

_____

Christianity is radical. Jesus demands everything. He demands that we die to ourselves and live for Him. Jan Silvious of Precept Ministries says that she had a defining moment in her life at the age of twenty-five when the Spirit showed her, like a bolt of lightning: *It's not about you, Jan.* She said, "It was at that point I gave all I knew of me to all I knew of God."[9]

D. Why is it important to count the cost before you make a commitment? What examples does Jesus give? (vv. 28–32)

_____

_____

E. Jesus also addresses the love of possessions in verse 33. In your opinion, why do you think that loving the world causes a Christian to lose her saltiness?

_____

_____

F. How do you respond to these warnings personally?

_____

_____

Just the Way You Look Tonight

In *When Christ Comes,* Max Lucado tells how, as a minister, he spends plenty of time with the nervous groom before the ceremony, watching him tug at his collar and mop his brow. Before the ceremony the groom may have been joking with his friends about escaping, but during the ceremony, especially at the moment when the bride enters, Max notices this as he sneaks a peek at the groom:

> If the light is just so and the angle just right, I can see a tiny reflection in his eyes. Her reflection. And the sight of her reminds him why he is here. His jaw relaxes and his forced smile softens. He forgets he's wearing a tux. He forgets his sweat-soaked shirt. . . . When he sees her, any thought of escape becomes a joke again. For it's written all over his face, "Who could bear to live without this bride?"[10]

The Lord loves you so much. You are His Bride, the object of His affection. And just as an earthly bridegroom is pleased by commitment, fidelity, and abandonment from his bride, that is what Jesus longs for from each of us.

A bride who demonstrates this perfectly is Ruth. She was a surprising bride, as a Moabitess, but she became an absolutely beautiful bride. As the Book of Ruth progresses, everyone is talking about her. Boaz told her, "All my fellow townsmen know that you are a woman of noble character" (Ruth 3:11). She abandoned herself to Naomi and to Naomi's God. Boaz also said to her, "You have put aside your personal desires" (Ruth 3:10b TLB). When a person lives this way, she is transformed; she is absolutely beautiful. Andrew Murray, in *Like Christ,* explains:

> This undivided surrender to follow Him is crowned with this wonderful blessing, that Christ by His Spirit becomes his life. . . . Christ has taken the place of self, and His love and gentleness and kindness flow out to others, now that self is parted with. No command becomes more blessed or more natural than this: "We ought not to please ourselves, for even Christ pleased not Himself." "If any man come after me, let him deny himself, and FOLLOW ME."[11]

In the Book of Ruth, both Orpah and Ruth, two young widows from Moab, are invited to follow the one true God. As they come to the crossroads of decision, with one road leading back to idol-worshipping Moab and the other to the Promised Land, they are warned repeatedly. There may be a high cost. If they go with Naomi to

Bethlehem, it is quite possible that no Jewish men will ever want to marry them, and they will remain single for the rest of their lives. Being a single woman in biblical days was especially difficult, for women were dependent on men for food and shelter. But Ruth abandons herself, falling back, believing Naomi's God will catch her.

Review your memory verses. A prayer I (Dee) have often sung is "Change My Heart, O God" (see Appendix A).

Read Ruth 1:1–2:16 as if you were reading a story.

THOMAS MATTHEW ROOKS (1842–?)[vi]

ᕤᕤ

This artist tells the story through a trifold mural. We believe he has captured Ruth's love for Naomi, her humility before Boaz, and her desire to fill up the empty arms of her mother-in-law.

15. What made Ruth stand out to Boaz and the people of Bethlehem? (Consider the words of Boaz and the words of Andrew Murray quoted in today's introduction.)

_____

_____

16. Read Ruth 1:6–14.

A. What does Naomi tell her daughters-in-law to do, and why? (vv. 8–9)

_____

_____

B. What is the initial response of Orpah and Ruth? (v. 10)

_____

C. How many more times does Naomi try to send them back, and how does she intensify her argument? (v. 11–13)

_____

_____

D. Describe the choice of each daughter-in-law. (v. 14) Put yourself in their shoes and try to imagine why each made the choice that she did.

_____

_____

E. On a symbolic level, Orpah and Ruth each represent the person at the crossroads of a spiritual decision for Christ. At that crossroads, the individual realizes there may be a cost in following Christ. What are some reasons individuals choose to retreat?

_____

_____

F. What are some reasons individuals choose to take the risk and abandon their lives to Christ?

_____

_____

17. After Orpah turns back, she falls out of the pages of Scripture and her name is never mentioned again. In contrast, find a phrase in each of the following passages to see how Ruth is remembered.

A. Ruth 2:11_____

B. Ruth 3:11_____

C. Ruth 4:15_____

D. Matthew 1:1 and 1:5_____

18. How do you think you will be remembered after your death? Why?

_____

_____

DAY 5

I'll Be Your Shelter

Shortly before Christmas 1996, Kathy wrote in her journal:

> *December 12, 1996*
>
> *I long to be awakened. I long to be touched in a place in my soul that I know God intended . . . I long to feel the inexpressible joy that comes from a woman in love. I long to be a bride.*
> *Please find me.*

What Kathy is longing for is a man who walks in the fear of a holy God. Truly godly men (and they are rare) are so different from most men. They are interested in you, they are great listeners, they are gifted in intimacy, and they are willing to make the hard choices that God requires of a person, because they love and trust Him. Kathy is longing for a Boaz to find her.

Hollywood would probably never capture the Book of Ruth. They'd likely add immorality to the story. They'd miss its beautiful symbolism. And they'd have difficulty grasping that the magnetism and charisma of Boaz came from his deep connection to God.

As you discover how Boaz wooed, won, and wed Ruth, remember that Boaz is a Christ figure. Glimmering beneath this man is Jesus, who loves you, who longs to be a shelter for you, not only in salvation, but each moment of your life.

As you consider Ruth, remember that she represents you, as a believer, as the Bride of Christ. Just as we have been redeemed, so was Ruth. She was ashamed of her past, having been a Moabite who worshipped detestable gods. Ruth felt unworthy of the kindness of Boaz, and yet she was profoundly thankful. As widows, she and Naomi were in great need. Women in Ruth's day could not own property. Essentially, they were dependent upon the kindness of others for food and shelter.

When Naomi and Ruth arrive in Bethlehem, Ruth asks permission of Naomi to go out and pick up leftover grain "behind anyone in whose eyes I find favor" (Ruth 2:2a). Naomi does not suggest that Ruth go to the field of Boaz, who is a near kinsman and a man of kindness and position. Naomi, still overcome by the grief of losing her husband and sons, cannot seem to manage more than, "Go ahead, my daughter" (Ruth 2:2b). Yet God, in His mercy, directs Ruth's steps to the field of Boaz.

To prepare your heart, go over Ruth 1:16–17 until it is sealed in your mind and heart.

19. Naomi had probably taught her daughter-in-law about the "mercy" laws. Now Naomi and Ruth are about to benefit from two of these laws. Describe each of them.

A. Deuteronomy 24:19–21 _____

_____

B. Deuteronomy 25:5–6 _____

_____

Boaz was not an immediate brother, but a near kinsman. The tie is close enough to be significant. You can almost hear the violins begin to play by the way Boaz is introduced in chapter 2.

20. Read Ruth 2:1–16.

    A. In each verse of Ruth 2:1–5, find an indication of building suspense, a phrase or hint that romance is waiting in the wings.

        (v. 1)_____

        (v. 2)_____

        (v. 3)_____

        (v. 4)_____

        (v. 5)_____

    B. What is Boaz told about the character of Ruth? (vv. 6–7)

_____

    C. Find all the evidences of Boaz's chivalry in Ruth 2:8–9. In each instance, how can you see Jesus glimmering through?

_____

_____

_____

    D. Describe Ruth's response. (v. 10) Why do you think she was surprised?

_____

_____

    E. How has Boaz seen "abandonment" and character in Ruth? (v. 11)

_____

_____

    F. Imagine Jesus praying the prayer of Boaz (v. 12) over you. In what ways might Jesus have seen abandonment in you?

_____

_____

G. How can you see that Ruth is encouraged, yet still amazed? (v. 13)

_____

_____

H. How does Boaz continue to show chivalry? (vv. 14–16)

_____

_____

What a guy! How we love to be treated so tenderly by men. Once we come into a relationship with Jesus we often are willing, if we were not before, to be treated with chivalry.

January 29, 2000

> *If I had not fallen in love with you, Lord, I would probably be a militant feminist . . . You've brought me so much balance—each year you teach me more and more about what it means to be your woman, while you allow me to get glimpses of your heart in some of the men that cross my path . . .*
>
> *Much to my surprise I've arrived at a place of loving and even yearning for chivalry . . . I feel like royalty when a door is held open for me, when a chair is pushed back for me, and when a hand reaches to help me out of a car.*
>
> *I pray that I will know in this life what it means to be treated like a princess by a man whom you have called to be my prince.*

21. Do you appreciate the kind of chivalry that you see in Boaz? What do you like or don't you like? Have you shared this with a man in your life?

_____

_____

When we meet men who pray passionately, who walk in the fear of a holy God, who continually choose the highest path, and who radiate His love and, yes, His chivalry, we catch a glimpse of Jesus. Boaz certainly radiates the Lord, but the picture we are given of Boaz is deeper than that. He is a "kinsman-redeemer" who is meant to illustrate a beautiful picture. We will return to this story, but it is important to know that just as Boaz was a "kinsman-redeemer" to Ruth, Jesus is a "kinsman-redeemer" to you.

22. According to 1 Peter 1:18, from what did Jesus redeem you? What was the price?

_____

_____

23. Think of a few ways Jesus has been a shelter to you.

_____

_____

24. Can you identify with Ruth's feelings in Ruth 2:10 and 2:13? Explain.

_____

_____

Close your quiet time today by giving thanks to the Lord for being your Bridegroom, your Boaz, your kinsman-redeemer.

Finale

REVIEW

25. Each woman should share, if she chooses, one way she was "kissed by the King" in this study.

PRAYER

We are all in the process of abandoning ourselves to Christ. Even though we may have had, as Jan Silvious expressed it, a moment when we gave all that we knew of ourselves to all that we knew of God, we are soon to discover there is more to God, and more of ourselves to give. In what ways is His Spirit encouraging you to be more abandoned? Cluster in groups of no larger than five and bravely lift this up to the Lord and allow the other group members to support you. When there is a silence, the next woman who has the courage should lift the area in which she desires to be more abandoned. For example:

> *Amy:* I need to relinquish my concerns over my adult son to You, Lord. Help me to give him to You and leave him in Your arms.
> *Ellen:* I agree, Lord.
> *Lori:* When anxious thoughts come to Amy, Lord, help her to relinquish Rob to You again.
> *Ellen:* Please work in Rob's heart and life.
> *Jean:* I agree, Lord.
> Silence
> *Lori:* I have a secret sin to which I am tempted to return. Please help me.
> *Amy:* O Lord, give Lori strength.
> *Jean:* Help her to see clearly the lies of the enemy, that this sin will bring her comfort. Help her to see the true picture, the devastation ahead.
> *Amy:* I agree, Lord. Help our sister Lori. Give her the desire to be true to You.
> Silence

Softly close with "Change My Heart, O God" (see Appendix A).

WEEK 5

Love Me Tender

Prelude

My (Dee's) favorite real-love romance is told in the book *A Severe Mercy*. This story of a shining young couple captured the award for *Christianity Today's* book of the year in 1977. The love of this couple was profound, and intriguing, for it involved the story of their conversion to Christ through their friendship with C. S. Lewis. Sheldon Vanauken (Van) described how he felt during his first date with Jean Davis (Davy):

> Her eyes, I had not failed to observe, were indeed beautiful: long eyes, grey eyes with a hint of sea-green in certain lights. A wide brow and a small determined chin—a heart-shaped face. Rather suddenly, without previous reflection on the matter, it began to appear to me that heart-shaped faces were perhaps the best. . . .
>
> We talked and looked at each other by firelight, for I had switched out the lamps. She told me about a coasting voyage she had taken all by herself, just because she wanted to be on a ship and the sea. . . . There had been a storm . . . she had crept forward into the bow and crouched in a coil of line, wet and loving the spray and the plunging bow. This story appealed to me beyond words. Then we discovered we each loved poetry, she capped one of my quotations. We grinned at each other. . . .
>
> One who has never been in love might mistake either infatuation or a mixture of affection and sexual attraction for being in love. But when the "real thing" happens, there is no doubt. . . . So with Davy and me. A sudden glory.[1]

In the same way, when you are persuaded—through the prophecies, or the miracles, or the changed lives of others—that Jesus is, indeed, who He claimed to be, when you come into a personal relationship with Him, when His Spirit bears witness with your spirit, you are overwhelmed by the "sudden glory." All religious leaders from the beginning of time suddenly pale in comparison to Jesus. Confucius, Buddha, Mohammed—they were just men. Gifted men, but now, dead men. They were not God. No one can compare to Jesus. Why?

Jesus alone is God. Jesus alone lives. Jesus alone could truthfully say:

Whoever drinks the water I give him will never thirst. Indeed, the water
I give him will become in him a spring of water welling up to eternal life.
(John 4:13)

I am the resurrection and the life. He who believes in me will live, even though
he dies; and whoever lives and believes in me will never die. (John 11:25)

I am the way and the truth and the life. No one comes to the Father
except through me. (John 14:6)

I am the vine; you are the branches. If a man remains in me and I in him,
he will bear much fruit; apart from me you can do nothing. (John 15:5)

Jesus is the One for whom we were made. We were created to be loved by Him. And we were created to love Him with all of our heart, with all of our mind, and with all of our soul.

WATCH VIDEO #5: LOVE ME TENDER

Dee will be teaching from Luke 10:38–42.

OPTIONAL NOTE-TAKING SPACE

_____

_____

_____

_____

_____

_____

GROUP RESPONSE TO THE VIDEO

A. What similarities did Dee see between her first-love time with her husband and her first-love time with Jesus? Could you identify? If so, how?

B. How did Dee describe Mary of Bethany? Martha?

C. Why did Jesus rebuke Martha? What did He mean by His words in Luke 10:42?

D. What thoughts did you have concerning the story Kathy told about dancing with Jesus? What message is there in this story for you personally?

I Feel the Earth Move

Van describes how he and his wife felt during that first-love time:

> There was in both of us a kind of hesitant, incredulous wonder. Could this really be happening—this marvel?
>
> . . . The actual thing—inloveness—requires something like a spark leaping back and forth from one to the other becoming more intense every moment, love building up like voltage in a coil.[2]

Likewise, when you are in your first-love time with Jesus, there is an "incredulous wonder" and a spark leaps back and forth. Even though I still had laundry, dishes, and a fussy baby, my (Dee's) life during that first-love time was so interesting. I was serving Him. I had a sense that *He* might intervene and quiet my baby, or speak to me through *His* Spirit or *His* Word, or surprise me with some divinely orchestrated circumstance. My heart was so full. I couldn't believe my perspective was so different. I wanted to stop people in the grocery store, to stand up on the city bus, and say to all those weary faces: "Don't you know? Jesus is real! He has changed my life—and He can change yours!"

Just as I had listened carefully to Steve during our first dates, looking for signs of his love, fascinated by his mind, I listened intently again. Only now, I was actually listening to the One who made the universe, and He cared about *me* and had wisdom for *my* individual life. Before, the Bible had seemed boring and hard to understand. Now, it was the living Word of God!

I was in my first-love time.

We will begin to look at the Song of Songs this week. Christ is hidden in almost every page of the Bible, but it is in this book, Charles Spurgeon says, that "we see his heart and feel his love to us."[3] Matthew Henry comments that it is fitly placed after the Book of Ecclesiastes, for it is its opposite. Instead of the saddest song, that vanity of vanities of looking for love in all the wrong places, it is the sweetest song, the song of Christ's love for His Bride and our love for Him.[4]

Many Christians are uncomfortable with the Song of Songs on the metaphorical level because they simply cannot believe that Jesus loves them the way Solomon loved the Shulammite maiden. If you are uncomfortable with this, perhaps it is because you have not yet experienced the sweet delight of intimacy that Jesus longs for you to know. Hundreds of years ago, in commenting on the Song of Songs, Joseph Irons wrote that many believers are:

not likely to esteem this book as it ought to be esteemed; only those who have lived near to Jesus . . . only those who know the fullness of the word "communion," can sit down to this book with delight and pleasure; and to such men these words are as wafers made with honey, manna, angels' food: every sentence is like gold, and every word is like much fine gold.[5]

Charles Spurgeon, the mighty "Prince of Preachers" of the nineteenth century, loved the Song of Songs, explaining:

If I must prefer one book above another, I would prefer some books of the Bible for doctrine, some for experience, some for example, some for teaching, but let me prefer this book above all others for fellowship and communion. When the Christian is nearest to heaven, this is the book he takes with him.[6]

Begin memorizing Song of Songs 1:2:

Let him kiss me with the kisses of his mouth—
for your love is more delightful than wine. (Song of Songs 1:2)

1. What stood out to you from this week's Prelude or from today's introduction?

   _____

   _____

   _____

In the opening of chapter 2 of the Song of Songs, the Shulammite maiden is still in her first-love time. She is delighting in Solomon's love, and drinking in his words.

2. Read Song of Songs 2:1–7.

   A. What does the lover, who represents Jesus, say about His beloved, who represents us? (v. 2) What do you think this metaphor means?

   _____

   _____

   B. To what does the beloved compare her lover? (v. 3) Compare this with Hosea 14:8b. What do you learn from this metaphor?

   _____

   _____

   C. Describe the beloved's euphoria in verses 4 and 5.

Dwight L. Moody said there were times when he was so overwhelmed with the Lord's love that he felt he could not contain such torrents and so He asked the Lord to restrain the flow.[7]

_____

_____

3. If you have experienced a deep earthly love relationship with a man, perhaps a man who became your husband, describe what it was about him that drew you to him. Remember the height!

_____

_____

4. Describe what you were like in the way you related to this earthly love in your first-love time.

_____

_____

5. If you are married, how could you apply Revelation 2:4–5a so that you could improve your marriage? What goal could you set and be accountable for to your small group?

_____

_____

6. Recall what it was that drew you to Jesus. Write down whatever you remember.

_____

_____

_____

7. If you gave your life to Jesus as an adult, recall what you were like in your first-love time. If you came to Christ as a child, recall a time when you were old enough to be overwhelmed by the wonder of it all. What things did you do then that evidenced your love?

_____

_____

_____

8. How could you apply Revelation 2:4–5a to your relationship with Jesus? What goal could you set and be accountable for to your small group?

_____

_____

Kiss Me

A kiss on the mouth is very intimate. I (Dee!) will never forget Steve's first kiss. I had wondered when he would kiss me for the first time. I remember exactly where we were, the trench coat he was wearing, the way he looked at me. I remember thinking, *Oh my—this is it—he's going to kiss me.* Then he lifted my chin gently with his hand and leaned down.

I spent the next few days in a daze. Most of you are too young to have seen *South Pacific*, but it is a classic worth renting. I felt like Nellie, played by Mitzi Gaynor, who danced around on the beach singing "I'm in Love with a Wonderful Guy."

The Hebrew word translated "kiss" in the Song of Songs is *nasaq,* meaning "to kindle, to catch fire." That first kiss may light a fire and bring the relationship to a new level of intimacy.

In the opening of the Song of Songs, the Shulammite maiden says:

> Let him kiss me with the kisses of his mouth—
> for your love is more delightful than wine. (Song of Songs 1:2)

Watchman Nee explains:

> Her former relationship with the Lord was a mere ordinary one which she felt to be most unsatisfactory. Now she longs for a far more intimate and personal relationship. She yearns, therefore, for His kisses, which would show His own ardent and personal love for her.[8]

What is a kiss from the King? What is a kiss from Jesus?

A kiss is a way of expressing love. God shows us His love in many ways, but three common ways are through:

- His **presence**
- His **provisions**
- His **prophecies**

His presence gives us peace in the midst of the storms of life, comfort in sorrow, and a joy the world cannot take away. His provisions are manifold: the rising sun, a flaming red ball peaking majestically out from the eastern landscape; a kindred spirit, someone to whom you can confide your innermost soul; and the precious gift of a newborn baby, plump with possibility. His prophecies are the living words of

Scripture sent from His heart to our heart. Jamie Lash and her husband are the directors of a Messianic Jewish ministry that includes the national television program *Jewish Jewels*. Jamie spent two hours a day, for five years, meditating on the Song of Songs. In her book *A Kiss a Day*, she talks about how, according to rabbinical tradition, a kiss from God is a living word of prophecy.[9] Have you ever had the experience of a verse from the Bible jumping off the page at you, and knowing that it was a word from God to you? If so, you've been kissed by the King.

Recently I (Kathy) looked at the big, thick Bible I had in the late seventies. It made me laugh to see how I had highlighted it. Ephesians and Romans are just one blob of yellow. I chuckled and thought, *All of it was such a revelation. I highlighted it all.* I was experiencing the ecstasy of kisses from the King.

Continue memorizing Song of Songs 1:2.

9. What is a kiss from the King? What is it, according to rabbinical tradition?

_____

_____

10. Can you remember a recent "kiss," a "living word of prophecy" that awakened you or comforted you? If so, share what it was.

_____

_____

11. Meditate on Song of Songs 1:2.

A. *Let him kiss me*
   What significance do you see in the fact that she is asking for her lover's kisses? How could you apply this to the times you have with the Lord in His Word?

_____

_____

B. *with the kisses of his mouth*
   What significance do you see in a "kiss of his mouth" in contrast to a kiss on the hand or the cheek?

_____

_____

C. The root Hebrew word for kiss is *nasaq*, meaning "to kindle, to catch fire." Can you think of an example of when the Word of God lit a fire in you?

_____

_____

D. Compare "Let him kiss me with the kisses of his mouth" to Psalm 119:17–20. What is the psalmist asking for? How do you think he will respond if God grants him his request?

_____

_____

E. *for your love*
    She opened this verse in the third person ("Let *him*") as she was talking about him to her friends, the daughters of Jerusalem. Now she moves to the more intimate second person ("*your* love"). Why do you think she does this?

_____

F. *is more delightful than wine*
    What does wine do that is similar to kisses from the King? (See Psalm 104:15a.)

_____

_____

_____

G. How does wine fall short of the pleasure of intimacy with Jesus, of kisses of the King? (See Ecclesiastes 2:1-3 for wine in moderation and Proverbs 23:29–35 for wine in excess.)

_____

_____

DAY 3

Kisses Sweeter Than Wine

The person who is in her first-love time with Jesus, or the person who is falling more deeply in love with Jesus, views His Word like kisses, kisses like honey to her mouth (Psalm 119:103). Psalm 119 is the longest psalm, the psalm exalting the Word of God, and a psalm written by a man whom C. S. Lewis described as being "ravished by moral beauty."[12] One of the main ways we are kissed by the King is through His "prophecies." The person deeply in love with Jesus is also deeply in love with His

Word. She marvels at its order, its beauty, and its power. She longs to be with Jesus, to slip away with Him, and to immerse herself in His Word.

In the Song of Songs, the Shulammite maiden says: "Your love is more delightful than wine" (Song of Songs 1:2b). The word for *love* in the Hebrew is *dodim* or, literally, "caresses." Ask the Lord for His caresses as you study His Word today.

12. Gaze on a few of the pearls on the lovely necklace of Psalm 119.

A. According to Psalm 119:1–2, how can the Word of God bless you? (Remember the definition of *blameless* from Day 3 of Week 2.)

_____

_____

B. In Psalm 119:32, what does the psalmist say the Word of God has done for him? Can you think of an example of how the Word has done this for you?

_____

_____

C. Where does the psalmist find comfort in his suffering? (Psalm 119:50) What does he ask God to do? (Psalm 119:49)

_____

_____

D. Describe the longing of the psalmist for God's kisses. (Psalm 119:145–148)

_____

_____

> God's promises are his bonds. . . . He loves that we should wrestle with him by his promises.[13]
>
> —Richard Sibbes
> (1577–1635)

Another way to be "kissed by the King" is through His provisions. After my (Kathy's) struggles with bulimia and during my mother's illness, I took a break from singing. I had no money. When I first got back into the limelight, I was working really hard, yet receiving little income. My parents were gone, I didn't have a husband, and I started to think, *Who's going to take care of me?*

Shortly after that I did a concert in Phoenix. A couple whom I had briefly met a few years earlier came up to me before I went onstage. The husband said, "Kathy, we've prayed about this and we really feel like we want to bless you. We want to give you fifty thousand dollars."

I thought, *What? Did I hear him right?* So I asked, "What do you mean?"

He repeated, "We want to give you fifty thousand dollars."

I said, "Well, as a loan . . . when do I have to pay you back?"

He said, "No, Kathy. It's a gift. Our only requirement is that you keep on sharing the gospel the way you do."

Needless to say, I was completely overwhelmed. A tender kiss from the King.

13. List a few ways the Lord has kissed you through provisions in the last year. Think particularly about friendship, financial provisions, and beautiful scenery. List these things, giving thanks to Him as you do.

_____

_____

The Lord also kisses us through His presence. Do you remember how amazing it was to experience that as a new believer?

I (Dee) definitely had the sense that I was not alone anymore. I found myself talking to Jesus, singing to Him. Our little boys soon were singing too: "Oh, how I love Jesus. Oh, how I love Jesus. . . ." There was a melody in our hearts, for He was so near. I had a sense of belonging to Someone.

And I (Kathy), as a single woman, didn't feel as alone anymore. One of my favorite verses, because it's so intimate, so caressing, and so enveloping of me as a woman, is:

> His left arm is under my head,
>   and his right arm embraces me. (Song of Songs 2:6)

14. Share a time when you experienced His presence.

_____

_____

Do you remember the commercial for the fragrance Windsong? *Her Windsong stayed on his mind.* Fragrance makes us aware of the sweet presence of a person. Fragrances in biblical days were used frequently, and Eastern people placed a high value on them. Weary travelers were hospitably welcomed by having their feet bathed and rubbed with soothing ointment. Oils were used for medicinal and healing purposes. And precious fragrances were used to anoint those to whom special honor was to be shown.

Psalm 45 is a Messianic wedding song. Concerning the bridegroom, we are told:

> All your robes are fragrant with myrrh and aloes and cassia. (Psalm 45:8a)

Likewise, in the Song of Songs, the Shulammite says of the bridegroom:

> Pleasing is the fragrance of your perfumes;
>   your name is like perfume poured out.
>   No wonder the maidens love you! (Song of Songs 1:3)

15. Share a time when you experienced His presence.

A. The fragrance of myrrh was associated with suffering and death. It was used to anoint bodies. The Shulammite says, "Your name is like perfume poured out." Discover the meaning of the name *Jesus* in Matthew 1:21 and then explain how the name *Jesus* is associated with myrrh.

_____

_____

B. Aloes and cassia were used in healing. When God loosed Zechariah's tongue after the birth of John the Baptist, Zechariah said Jesus was the rising sun that would come to us from heaven. This was a fulfillment of Malachi 4:2: "For you who revere my name, the sun of righteousness will rise with healing in its wings. And you will go out and leap like calves released from the stall." Explain several ways Jesus has brought healing to you.

_____

_____

C. "Therefore do the virgins love thee" (Song of Songs 1:3b KJV). If you are trusting in Christ, you are a virgin, you are clean in His sight. He has sacrificed for you and brought healing in His wings. Do you believe this? How does it make you feel toward Jesus?

_____

_____

As a young believer, I (Kathy) went to a church that shared communion each Sunday. (I happen to be a fan of sharing communion every week.) Every time communion was passed, I sobbed. It was to the point where people would come over to me, put their arms around my shoulders, and try to bring me comfort. I knew they were wondering if something was wrong. Nothing was wrong. In fact, everything was right. I had been awakened to who Jesus was and what He had done for me. I had been invited into His presence, though I was so undeserving. I realized He truly loved me. It would simply break my heart each time I thought about it. For a number of months my tears became part of the service. People just expected it. They began to understand that I was overwhelmed by my newfound Love. When new people would come toward me to offer comfort, they would get stopped by the regulars, who would whisper, "She's okay. That's just Kath. She cries during communion."

I Only Have Eyes for You

The first-love time is incredibly sweet. When Anna, the young widow in *The King and I*, sings "Hello, Young Lovers," she remembers poignantly the preciousness of being in love for the first time. She remembers what it felt like to have wings on her heels, for her heart to beat faster when her lover came into view.

Perhaps that's how Mary of Bethany felt each time Jesus appeared at her door.

The first time we meet Mary of Bethany is in a passage that is so familiar to women that we tend to skim over it, assuming we know what it says. Often, we are so focused on Martha that we miss Mary. Read the opening to this familiar passage, but this time concentrate on Mary:

> As they continued their travel, Jesus entered a village. A woman by the name of Martha welcomed him and made him feel quite at home. She had a sister, Mary, who sat before the Master, hanging on every word he said. But Martha was pulled away by all she had to do in the kitchen. (Luke 10.38–39 MSG)

Through His words, Mary was being kissed by the King. She was "hanging on every word he said." That's how it is when you first fall in love. You don't want to miss a word, a tender inflection, a warm look, a gentle kiss. All are precious. Mary could not imagine leaving His side.

Christ in the Home of Mary and Martha
JAN VEMEER (1863–1933)[vii]

୧ଓ

This famous painting by a Dutch master captures the tenderness of Jesus toward each of the sisters. Vemeer does not portray the disciples as present.

To prepare yourself for time with God, review your memory verse from Week 3 and this week's memory verse. You may want to use the following lyrics from "Help Myself to You," a song Kathy sang on one of her earliest albums, as a prayer to the Lord:

> Gonna close my door
> Gonna shut out the lights
> Want to be alone
> With you at my side
> Tell me all those things
> That I long to hear
> In that still small voice
> Whisper in my ear
> To be alone with you, Jesus
> It's such an honor for me
> Pour your life—into me
> Fill me with—your glory
> Let your love—consume me
> Oh to be at this place
> It's an act of your grace
> And there's nothing that I'd
> rather do
> Than to help myself to you

Though Mary is the silent figure in the passage today, she was not passive. Darrell Bock says that a woman sitting at the feet of a rabbi was most unusual. But the reflexive verb "sat at the Lord's feet" is literally "she sat herself beside." Mary took the initiative. Though she was a woman, she somehow knew He loved her and wanted to teach her. Bock writes:

> Jesus' ministry breaks molds. Those who are sensitive to him recognize that he invites them to come to him. They sense that he will receive them, that he is ready to teach all types of people.[15]

16. If you have a Bible map, look up Bethany. Note how close it is to Jerusalem and why this might be significant in the frequent travels of Jesus to Jerusalem.

_____

17. Read Luke 10:38–42.

A. *a woman named Martha opened her home to him*
   Who seems to own and run this home? What insight does this give you into the story?

_____

_____

This is interesting, as women were not allowed to own property. Tradition says that Simon the Leper (the man who threw the party after the raising of Lazarus in John 12) may have been related to these three siblings, either as their father or as the husband of Martha. However, as a leper, he did not live with them. Obviously, however, by the time Simon the Leper threw the party, he had been healed, probably by Jesus. Tradition also says they were a wealthy family, as evidenced by the worth of Mary's alabaster jar of perfume in John 12.

What evidence of a hospitable heart do you see in Martha?

_____

B. *She had a sister called Mary, who sat at the Lord's feet*
Note where Mary is in this "first-love" time. Compare this with her position in the "wilderness-love" time (John 11:32) and that "invincible-love" time (John 12:3). What does this tell you about Mary?

_____

_____

Mary took the initiative here, for the Greek is literally "she sat herself beside." What does this tell you about her heart? Compare her heart to David's heart in Psalm 42:1–2.

_____

_____

Women were treated as second-class citizens in the days of Jesus, and they were not supposed to sit at the feet of a rabbi. That was a privilege reserved for men. That might have played a part in Martha's thinking. But how does Jesus protect Mary? (Luke 10:42) What does this tell you?

_____

_____

C. *listening to what he said*
The Message paraphrases this as "hanging on every word he said." What could you learn from Mary for your own times with the Lord?

_____

_____

D. *But Martha was distracted by all the preparations that had to be made*

Describe Martha's frame of mind, contrasting her to Mary. Note also how Jesus describes Martha in Luke 10:41.

_____

_____

The word *distracted* contains the concept of divided attentions. It occurs again in 1 Corinthians 7:32–35, where we are told that one of the advantages of remaining single is that we will not be so distracted, but can live in "undivided devotion" to the Lord. What tends to divide your attention from the Lord?

_____

_____

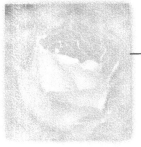

DAY 5

All Shook Up

She was the Martha Stewart of biblical days. Can't you just see Martha stenciling the disciples' lunch bags with daisies, fussing over fresh fish crepes with lemon sauce, carving soap into heart shapes, and placing bayberry candles in the window? And when the Master came, the same kind of crazy hormones that fall upon us as women in December fell upon Martha. All stops were unleashed. The house had to be at its best, the meal had to be a gourmet experience—nothing was too good for Jesus.

Some artists depict this scene with all of the disciples in the room along with Mary, seated around Jesus, and poor Martha alone at the door to the kitchen, cheeks flushed, her hands on her hips in anger. As women, we tend to sympathize with Martha. Fixing lunch for thirteen men who show up without notice is *not* a one-woman job.

But notice the pronouns in Luke 10:38 carefully: "As Jesus and his disciples were on their way, *he* came to a village where a woman named Martha opened her home to *him*" (italics added). Hmm—is it possible Jesus was alone? That's how Walter Wangerin interprets it in *The Book of God:*

> During these last three years He has usually come in the company of His
> disciples. He first makes sure they all have food and places to sleep in
> Bethany. Then He silently slips into our courtyard.[16]

If Jesus was alone, what was all the hubbub about? A five-course meal beginning with bouillabaisse, homemade biscuits, and rosecut radishes? Charles Swindoll puts it like this: "Martha, Martha—chips and dip would be fine!"[17]

In *The Sacred Romance,* the authors claim that too often "communion with God is replaced by activity for God."[18] That is exactly what we see with Martha. Instead of communing with God, sitting at His feet and drinking in His words, she is anxiously bustling about with nervous energy, worried about many things. She had failed to guard her heart.

Martha had missed the best. Instead of communing with Jesus, she was in a whirl of activity, rushing from one task to another. Jesus gently rebuked Martha *because He loved her* and wanted the best for her. He was also protecting Mary *because He loved her* and did not want the best taken from her. How revolutionary! Surely most in that day would have thought any woman present belonged in the kitchen—not at the feet of a rabbi.

Cultivate the "Mary" in yourself by singing some praise choruses to Jesus, reviewing your memory verse, and then anticipating His kisses as you study your scripture.

Chinese Rendering of Mary and Martha with Jesus (1939)[viii]

෩

We liked this Chinese portrayal of Mary and Martha because it shows the universality of Jesus to every culture. Born at the corner of three worlds, with coloring that was probably a good mix of Asian, African, and Caucasian, He is truly a priest forever to all peoples, the Savior of the whole world.

18. Read Luke 10:38–42 again. Today we will concentrate on Martha.

    A. *She came to him and asked,*
       An admirable characteristic you will see repeatedly in Martha's life is that even when she was upset with the Lord, she kept dialoguing with Him. Why is it that in order to have a good marriage, whether to an earthly bridegroom or to our ultimate Bridegroom, we need to keep talking and we need to keep listening—even when we are upset?

_____

_____

It is also noteworthy, as you continue to study Martha's life in this guide, to see that every time Jesus answered her, even when He was chastening her, she listened. What does Proverbs 9:8–9 teach about this?

_____

_____

B. *"Lord, don't you care that my sister has left me to do the work by myself?*
Why is Martha upset with Jesus? What does she imply about His feelings for her?

_____

_____

How do you see Martha implying this same thing in John 11:21 and 11:39?

_____

_____

Are there times when you feel that way? What do you know about Jesus that could help you dispel that lie?

_____

_____

Why is Martha upset with her sister? What fundamental truth is Martha missing?

_____

_____

C. *Tell her to help me!"*
What does Martha envision Jesus will do?

_____

_____

Why do you think Martha felt so sure Jesus would support her in rebuking Mary?

_____

_____

D. *"Martha, Martha,"*

When Jesus says a name twice, it is usually accompanied by emotion and tenderness. How do you see this in Luke 13:34 and 22:31?

_____

_____

Why do you think Jesus viewed Martha tenderly?

_____

_____

E. *the Lord answered,*
   Every time Martha questioned the Lord, He answered her. What does this teach you about going deeper with Jesus? How does Jesus speak to us?

   _____

   _____

F. *"you are worried and upset about many things,*
   Jan Silvious believes that Martha wasn't just upset that day, she was generally upset. She had a "crowd in her mind." Because she had neglected the most important thing, which was sweet communion with Jesus, everything else had taken control. Do you have a "crowd in your mind"? What are some of the things you need to relinquish to Jesus?

   _____

   _____

G. *but only one thing is needed.*
   What is that one thing? See Revelation 2:2–5 to see Jesus giving a similar message to the church at Ephesus.

   _____

   _____

It isn't that Jesus doesn't value good deeds. He knows that good deeds will naturally flow out of communion with Him. But communion will not necessarily flow out of good deeds. There are a host of Christians who are busy with church activity, or just plain busy. They claim to love Jesus, but their time with Him, their aloneness with Him, their time to nurture their relationship with Him, has all but disappeared.

What is your "ministry" like when you neglect your communion with Jesus?

_____

_____

H. *Mary has chosen what is better,*

Is Jesus saying hospitality and service are wrong? If not, what is He saying? Explain.

_____

_____

I. *and it will not be taken away from her."*

What does it mean to you that, in a society that did not value women, Jesus defends the right of Mary to be at His feet?

_____

_____

Mary is often criticized, but she never defends herself. Why, do you think? (See 1 Peter 2:23.) What could you learn from this?

_____

_____

Finale

REVIEW

19. Each woman should share, if she chooses, one way she was "kissed by the King" in this study.

_____

_____

PRAYER

Pray conversationally in small groups. Instead of sharing prayer requests first, have each woman lift up her own request, and then have the other women support her.

ACT II

Wilderness Love

Orchestra
Adagio expressiva
(Play slowly, somberly, yet with grace)

WEEK 6

Killing Me Softly

Prelude

In the Song of Songs, the lover comes, leaping across the mountains, and invites his beloved to go higher with him:

Arise, my darling, my beautiful one, and come with me. (Song of Songs 2:10)

But she is content. She has camped out "in the clefts of the rock, in the hiding places on the mountainside" (2:14). At this point, she refuses to go higher with him, afraid of what it might involve.

So many women are like that. They are satisfied with where they are. They've gone so far with the Lord, and then they camp out in the hiding places. They're busy with Christian service, and they don't really want to surrender some of their hidden habits to Jesus. I (Kathy) often say, "We are as sick as our secrets." We end up doing things out of our brokenness instead of our wholeness. Jesus longs for us to live differently. He longs to set us free. There was a time when I weighed thirty-five pounds more than I do today. My weight didn't balloon up overnight. It was the result of poor choices. I allowed food to be my comfort. I could have camped out there. Poor eating habits are hard to break. But I thank God that the weight finally came off. It wasn't easy—it took a lot of hard work and discipline. It still takes discipline. But I want to live in such a way that I continually let Him take me to higher places.

Maybe you have developed unwise television habits or graceless ways of communicating with your sullen teenager, or maybe you haven't truly lived or shared your faith in front of other people for years. Maybe you've gotten lazy and complacent. You *are* a Christian, but you have camped out in a cleft of a rock while Jesus calls, "Take My hand and come higher." You are seemingly happy, but deep inside you are discontent. And with each call He makes, your heart grows sadder. You know you should heed His call, but you also know that change will be involved. That change can be painful.

If you are camped out in the hiding places, refusing to respond to God's Spirit, He will find you and begin to bring pain into your life, for "pain," C. S. Lewis says, "is God's megaphone." God begins gently, but if we do not respond, He will increase the pressure. The life of Jacob demonstrates how persistent God is in disciplining His erring children. Why? Because He loves us. We are the apple of His eye. He is on a quest for our love. He wants nothing less than complete abandonment.

This week's lesson is vital. If you are one who has trouble completing her lessons, determine in your heart that you will finish this week's lesson. You may want to do two days together early in the week to give yourself a head start.

WATCH VIDEO #6: KILLING ME SOFTLY

Dee will be teaching from the life of Jacob, beginning in Genesis 25.

OPTIONAL NOTE-TAKING SPACE

_____

_____

_____

_____

_____

GROUP RESPONSE TO THE VIDEO

A. What are some ways that God went about changing Jacob's heart?

B. What stood out to you from this video?

C. Kathy compared changing a bad habit to changing the course of a mountain stream by piling rocks up. It takes time, it takes work, but it can be successful. How might you apply this to your life? Be specific about the rocks you must pick up.

DAY 1

Up Where We Belong

Hannah Hurnard's *Hinds' Feet in High Places* is an allegory of the Song of Songs. In this classic, a fawn named Much-Afraid overcomes her fears and learns how to go to the high places with the Chief Shepherd. He tells her that in order to go to the High Places, she must make the climb herself, though he will never be far from her. She pleads with him to carry her. Gently the Chief Shepherd responds:

> Much-Afraid, I could do what you wish. I could carry you all the way up
> to the High Places myself, instead of leaving you to climb there. But if I did,
> you would never be able to develop hinds' feet, and become my companion

where I go. If you will climb to the heights this once with the companions I have chosen for you, even though it may seem a very long and in some places a very difficult journey, I promise you that you will develop hinds' feet.[1]

Hesitantly, Much-Afraid agrees. Then the Chief Shepherd tells her he will give her two companions. When she's introduced to them, she learns that they are called Sorrow and Suffering!

> Poor Much-Afraid! Her cheeks blanched and she began to tremble from head to foot.
> "Why, oh why, must you make Sorrow and Suffering my companions? Couldn't you have given me Joy and Peace? . . . I never thought you would do this to me!" Then she burst into tears.
> "Will you trust me, Much-Afraid?"[2]

Bad habits, especially those we have practiced for a lifetime, take drastic measures. Going higher *will* involve suffering. The Book of Hebrews compares our sinful ways to "broken bones." When you have a broken bone, your first visit to the doctor involves pain because he has to set the bone straight, sometimes even *rebreaking* it, so it can heal properly. If you camp out at home and say, "I'll just let nature take its course," your bone will heal improperly. You will be crippled for life. We must trust the Great Physician, even if the treatment, at first, is painful and difficult. One day we will be whole and able to climb to the high places.

Begin memorizing this week's memory verse:

> *No discipline seems pleasant at the time, but painful. Later on, however, it produces a harvest of righteousness and peace for those who have been trained by it.* (Hebrews 12:11)

1. What did you learn from this week's Prelude and today's introduction about camping out in the hiding places?

    _____

    _____

    _____

2. Read Song of Songs 2:8–14.

    A. How does the beloved describe the lover in verses 8–9?

    _____

    _____

    B. What does the lover now ask of the beloved? (vv. 10–13)

C. Where is she hiding? (v. 14)

_____

_____

D. Putting yourself in her place, what fears do you imagine kept her from going higher?

_____

_____

3. What fears keep you from going higher with the Lord? Meditate on your memory verse, and write yourself a mini-sermon here.

_____

_____

_____

You might want to pray through your above answer, asking the Lord to etch it on your heart, or you might want to sing "Change My Heart, O God" (see Appendix A) as a prayer.

Trying to Get the Feeling Again

After the Shulammite maiden refuses to leave her hiding place and come with her lover to the higher places, he goes to the higher places without her. She is lonely and sad. Desperately, she begins to look for him, asking others where he has gone. Tenderly, he knows how much she can bear, so he returns to her after a short absence. He lets her hold him in her "mother's house." But until she really leaves, she cannot fully cleave.

If we continue to camp out in the lower places, He will not stay with us, and we will begin to notice that the joy is gone, the peace has dissipated. We may be saved, but we are missing so much. At that point, we have two choices. We can try to restore our joy by running after the wrong things, by clinging to our idols, or we can return to the Lord and relinquish our idols. There isn't a middle road.

Jesus *is* incredibly patient and gentle with us. At the same time, He is strong and pointed about the things that cause us to commit adultery. God is a jealous God. He doesn't want us just to break the idols. He wants us to grind them into powder. This can seem frightening.

When God asks me (Kathy) to give something up, I put it in the closet or under the bed. The Lord says, "No." Then I throw it in my wastebasket. The Lord says . . . "No." Then I take it out to the street for the recycling pickup. The Lord says, "Absolutely not." Until I take my hammer and crush that idol into powder, it is still a temptation. The Lord's desire is for us to worship Him and Him alone.

When God took the Israelites through the wilderness, He was trying to teach them to let go of their idols. But instead of returning to the Lord, they tried to recapture those feelings of joy and peace that they had known during their marvelous deliverance by clinging to things under the sun and building gold idols. For years He was gentle with them, but then He increased the pain. Finally, He took their earthly lives from them, for we are told:

> God was not pleased with most of them; their bodies were scattered over the desert. Now these things occurred as examples to keep us from setting our hearts on evil things as they did. (1 Corinthians 10:5–6)

Review your memory verse.

4. What stood out to you from today's introduction? How might you apply it to your life?

_____

_____

_____

5. Read Psalm 106:6–23.

A. According to verses 7 and 13, what are root sins that we must guard against?

_____

_____

B. What are some ways you could build thankfulness and memory for God's goodness to you into your daily life?

_____

_____

C. What are some ways you could develop the habit of "waiting on the Lord's counsel" before you act?

_____

_____

6. Read Song of Songs 3:1–4.

   A. Describe the pain that the beloved feels when the lover leaves her. (vv. 1–3)

   _____

   _____

   B. Why do you think he left her if he loved her?

   _____

   _____

The pain of a loss of fellowship with the Lord is meant to bring us to our senses. But often, instead of forsaking our ways, we try to fill up that emptiness in another way.

7. Is it possible that you have lost the feelings you had when you first knew the Lord and have turned to pursuits under the sun, even to secret sins, in order to restore your joy and peace? Be as honest as you can with yourself, asking God to search your heart. What does He show you?

   _____

   _____

8. How do you see grace in Song of Songs 3:4?

   _____

   _____

9. From the following passages, what do you learn about God and how He works with us?

   A. Lamentations 3:31–33_____

   _____

   B. Lamentations 3:22–23_____

   _____

   C. Psalm 119:71_____

   _____

   D. Hebrews 12:5–11 _____

   _____

We did not sufficiently delight in the beauty of the Bridegroom when he did come to us; when our hearts were somewhat lifted up with his love we grew cold and idle, and then he withdrew his conscious presence; but, alas! We were not grieved, but we wickedly tried to live without him. . . . Jesus hides his face, the sun is set, and yet it is not night with you. Oh, may God be pleased to arouse you from this lethargy, and make you mourn your sad estate! Even if an affliction should be needed to bring you back from your backsliding it would be a cheap price to pay. Awake, O north wind, with all thy cutting force, if thy bleak breath may but stir the lethargic heart![3]

—Charles Spurgeon

DAY 3

You're a Hard Habit to Break

I (Kathy) see our carnal habits like a river running down a mountain. Every day, it goes down the same bank, runs along the same curves, and touches the same rocks. If we want to change the course of that river, it is going to take a lot of hard work and effort. It means first carrying the stones to the water and piling them one by one on top of each other. After a while the water will begin to flow in a new way because it's been redirected. Eventually there's a brand-new river bank and the water flows with ease on a new path. It takes time, it takes sacrifice, but it can be done and it will be worth it. I can't accept it when people say, "That's just the way I am." In Christ, we have the power to change. We must be the way *He* is.

There have been many changes I've needed to make in my life, new paths I've needed to follow. I'm definitely still in process. I struggle. I'm thankful for the victories I've had along the way.

For me, the first step has always been getting to the point where I am intolerant of my sin. My struggle with my weight is an example. I had to make the sacrifice of not eating when I wasn't hungry. If I had eaten a reasonable dinner, then I knew I didn't need to eat again before I went to bed. I had to let myself feel "a little hungry, a little lonely" when I turned in for the night. Jesus always gives us the grace to make right choices. We may be sad and discouraged, but His hand is always there to lead us to the foot of the cross where His blood can pour on us and we find new life.

I didn't lose weight overnight. It took time for my river to change its course. This new river is now a place of rejoicing for me.

I've kept my weight off for twelve years now. Whenever I go up five pounds, I remind myself of the pain I felt being overweight. I was always self-conscious when I walked into a room. I hardly ever wore a bathing suit. I agonized over the thought of going out to dinner for fear of the choices I'd make. I hated not being able to tuck my shirt in. It's not hard for me to remember how much pain I used to live in. It's all about choices, and I'm still faced with them every day. Do I have the desire to overeat? Absolutely! But I know what comes with that choice. And the freedom I've experienced in this particular struggle in my life is far better than having that constant ache in my soul.

I (Dee), too, am in process. But I so identify with Kathy's analogy of carrying the stones to change the course of a river. As a young mother, our firstborn, J. R., was a toddler who was in control of our home. He was disobedient and disrespectful, and I had not checked the flow. I remember how desperately he needed a nap, but I was at a loss as to how to keep him in his bed. Because he was so tired, he was constantly crying. My response? Sometimes I would simply cry with him. I was behaving, as author Jan Silvious puts it, like a "little girl Christian" instead of a "grown-up Christian." I was avoiding the difficult path of disciplining my child.

By the time J. R. was five, his river of disobedience was flowing forcefully. Eagerly I put him in a Christian school, and thanked God for the break. But the teacher, a godly older woman, called me in after two days and said:

> Mrs. Brestin—we do not take problem children in our school.

I began to cry. She came over and put her arms around me.

> Honey, I'm going to help you. We will give you six weeks to train J. R. to respect authority.

Then she gave me some child-training tapes explaining that I needed to prayerfully choose and set boundaries and keep them, and that if my child disobeyed, I needed to spank. I was horrified, at first, of the idea of spanking my child, even though I knew the Scripture said that if I spared the rod I would spoil the child. However, these tapes enlightened me, saying I must not spank the way the world spanks (in anger), but the way a woman controlled by the Spirit of God spanks (in love, with regret, and out of obedience to God in order to train the child). I began to approach discipline with a completely different spirit, and J. R. sensed it at once. It wasn't easy to train him to respect me. And it wasn't easy to allow myself to be trained by the Spirit of God. There were times when my son disobeyed me and I was tempted simply to ignore him. But then I pictured that river—I needed to train it to flow a new way. I had to pick up the stones and carry them to the river—not just once, but consistently, minute after minute, hour after hour, day after day. If I let nature run its course, I was going to ruin my son's life.

> Discipline your son in his early years while there is hope.
> If you don't you will ruin his life. (Proverbs 19:18 TLB)

As I persistently obeyed God as a mother, my son began to obey and respect me. In time, motherhood became a place of rejoicing for me.

> Discipline your son, and he will give you peace; he will bring delight to your soul. (Proverbs 29:17)

Today J. R. is a man who loves the Lord deeply and is in full-time Christian ministry. When he learned to obey and respect his parents, it prepared him to learn to obey and respect his Lord.

Kathy and I each have had many rivers that needed to be trained to run a new course. It was never easy, it was never without hard work, and it was never without pain. But when the river learned a new course, it was a place of great rejoicing.

Have we arrived? No, there are still many rivers that need to be redirected. But we are learning that if we are willing to die to ourselves, to go, as the Song of Songs puts it, to "the mountain of myrrh" (myrrh represents death and dying to ourselves), rejoicing will follow.

Review your memory verse.

10. What stood out to you from today's introduction?

_____

_____

11. Name a river in your life that you need to train to run a new course. What action do you need to take? What stones do you need to keep carrying to the river to redirect the flow?

_____

_____

12. Meditate on Hebrews 12:1–13.

A. What are we told to do in Hebrews 12:1?

_____

_____

B. In your life, what is a sin that easily entangles you? What are some of the natural consequences of that sin that God might allow you to experience?

_____

_____

C. What could you learn from the model of Jesus that could help you? (vv. 2–4)

_____

_____

D. What are two errors, on opposite poles, we must avoid when God disciplines us? (v. 5)

_____

_____

E. Why does God discipline us? (vv. 6–10) How should we respond?

_____

_____

F. When you discipline yourself in the area of the sin that besets you, what pain do you experience? What is vital to remember? (v. 11)

_____

_____

G. What word picture is given to show the importance of training your "weak knees" and "lame limbs"?

_____

_____

13. Meditate on Song of Songs 4:6–9.

A. Where is the Lover going? (v. 6) What does this represent? In verse 8, he is asking his bride, again, to come with him. How can you tell, from verse 9, that she has accepted this time?

_____

_____

Solomon's name means "peace" and the Shulammite's name means "in complete peace." The goal of our lives should be to come into complete peace with Jesus by abandoning all of our old ways of life. In an article entitled *The Kisses of the King*, Jackie Rodriguez writes:

> The Shulammite is the one for whom Jesus is looking. She is a bride who is not content with a momentary spiritual experience. Those who live only on past experiences take refuge in carnal religion that controls the soul. But the Shulammite was seeking to have an ongoing, intimate relationship with her beloved husband. . . .[3]

B. Do you feel you are living on past spiritual experiences or that you are seeking an ongoing, intimate relationship with Jesus? Explain.

_____

_____

C. How does Solomon respond to the Shulammite maiden? (v. 7) How will Jesus respond to you if you are willing to die to yourself in the area of your besetting sin?

_____

_____

If you have an hour sometime today, read Genesis 25:21 through Genesis 33. If you have a modern paraphrase, read that. Curl up and consider the fascinating life of Jacob.

DAY 4

You Always Hurt the One You Love

Following my (Dee's) recent knee surgery, I needed physical therapy. My physical therapist was a young man named Jacob. When I met him, I said, "Jacob. Now there's a strong biblical name."

Jacob lit up, enjoying the attention.

I continued, teasing him: "Jacob was a cheat and a liar, you know."

He smiled sheepishly. "Didn't he turn out okay in the end?"

I laughed. "You are absolutely right!"

Jacob grinned.

"But," I continued, ominously, "Jacob resisted giving God control of his life for one hundred years. He had a miserable life, and so did his whole family."

"Really," Jacob said, thoughtfully.

Since I had this young Jacob's attention, I continued. "Jacob tried to use God for his own agenda. God gave him everything, loved him, and promised to be with him, yet Jacob wanted to keep his hands on the reins of his life. Be sure you don't make that mistake, Jacob—or you will miss the wonderful life God has planned for you."

If we are honest, we will all admit that we are like Jacob. We have not appreciated the love of God, we have taken Him for granted, and we may even have tried to use Him for our own selfish purposes. Jacob's name means "he shall grab by the heel." Evangelist Luis Palau says that since Jacob spent his life climbing the ladder of success, that should be fair warning to "Watch out above! Watch out below!"[6]

It began, amazingly, in the womb. "In the womb," Hosea tells us, "[Jacob] grasped

(Isaac, Rebekah and Jacob)
Jacob Obtains by Fraus Isaac's Blessing
GOVEART FLINCK (1615–1660)[ix]

༕

The darkness of the painting portrays the darkness of the deed. Note Rebekah, who helped in the deception, in the background.

his brother's heel" (Hosea 12:3). Jacob spent his youth trying to get what rightfully belonged to Esau, "the blessing of the firstborn."

Together, Rebekah, Jacob's mother, and Jacob himself cheated Esau out of his birthright.

How interesting to see that the wicked act of Rebekah and Jacob was repeated, in a slightly different tune, years later by Laban, Leah's father, and Leah herself—only this time, it was Jacob who was the recipient of the pain. With the help of her father, Leah dressed up like her sister in order to steal, by deceit, what rightfully belonged to her sister.

God loved Jacob and wanted to take him to the higher places and make him holy. He was going to break Jacob's heart to get his attention. Rachel, an absolutely breathtaking woman, was part of God's plan.

Jacob and Rachel
WILLIAM DYCE (1806–1864)[x]

☙

The artist truly captured Jacob's adoration of Rachel.

I (Kathy) often reflect on how God woos me, wins me, and loves me to Himself. Many, many times He works on my heart by breaking my heart. I can't seem to learn any other way. I recently wrote a song with this chorus:

> It's been the rain,
> It's been the storms
> It's been the days when I've been worn
>
> That I have found you Lord
> That I have seen you Father
>
> It's in the pain
> That I have grown
> Through all the sorrow I have known
>
> But if that's what it takes
> For you to lead me this far
> Go ahead and break my heart

Review your memory verse.

14. What has pain in your life taught you recently?

_____

_____

15. Consider the following highlights of Jacob's youth:

A. Genesis 27:24–26
Jacob means "grabber" or "supplanter," or "he shall grab by the heel." How was this natural bent evidenced in Jacob's birth?

_____

_____

B. Genesis 27:1–10
The "blessing" for the firstborn was a prophetic prayer filled with great spiritual blessings. It is ironic that Jacob used deceit to get a blessing from God. Who helped him deceive his brother? How did the two of them plan this deceit?

_____

_____

C. Genesis 27:30–36
Describe Esau's grief at being tricked. Why do you think he was in such anguish?

_____

_____

D. Genesis 27:41–43
What natural consequence followed the deceit of Jacob and Rebekah?

_____

_____

It amazes me (Dee) that God didn't discipline Jacob more severely. And I am amazed at God's kindness to Jacob when he fled to Haran. I think, *Lord, why were You so kind to such a cheat and a liar?* And then I realize that it is because of His mercies that *I* am not consumed. I am so thankful that He has not treated *me* as my sins deserve. Many times He has offered me His kindness in hopes of leading me to repentance.

16. Consider how gently God began to deal with Jacob.
A. Genesis 28:10–15

Describe God's goodness to Jacob.

_____

_____

B. Genesis 28:16–17
Describe Jacob's initial response to the goodness of God.

_____

_____

C. Genesis 28:20–22
Describe the secondary response. What conditions does Jacob insist upon before he will allow God to be his God?

_____

_____

What Jacob tried to do was sign a prenuptial agreement with God. Instead of for better for worse, for richer for poorer, in sickness and health, Jacob would follow God for better, for richer, and for health. And if God reneged? Then Jacob planned to as well Just one catch. You can't sign a prenuptial agreement with the Almighty God.

17. Consider how God began to increase the pain in Jacob's life when he arrived at his Uncle Laban's farm.

A. Read Genesis 29:16–25.
How did Laban deceive Jacob?

_____

_____

What similarities do you see between the trick Jacob and his mother played on Esau and the trick Leah and her father played on Jacob?

_____

_____

B. Read Genesis 29:25–27.
Describe Jacob's anger. Imagine his thoughts and his feelings.

_____

_____

When we see the ugliness of sin in someone else, why might it be good to

I find the word if very interesting. Like the rest of us, Jacob had a lot to learn about covenant with God—that we cannot control the terms of the contract or the circumstances of our lives, and that once we claim the Lord as our God, we belong to Him and not vice-versa.[7]

—Leslie Williams

consider if there might be a similar sin in our own lives? Have you ever done this? If so, explain.

_____

_____

Pain may or may not be a result of sin. But it is always good to consider if that is a possibility, especially when you are having trouble getting along with people. If you have pain in a relationship, it is always good to ask if your choices in relating to this person have been the kind of choices Jesus would have made.

DAY 5

All I Ask of You

God asks us to repent. That means abandoning our sin, whatever that is in our lives, and trusting Him. Remorse isn't going to accomplish anything. Remorse is sadness without change. In Hosea, the Lord cried:

> *They do not cry out to me from their hearts*
> *but wail upon their beds.* (Hosea 7:14)

We don't want to do what it takes to repent. We don't want to change. We simply want to wail upon our beds. *Redeeming Love* is Francine River's retelling of the Book of Hosea. The adulterous wife, representing Gomer, has run away to her adulterous lover once again, and her husband, "Michael Hosea," comes after her. She locks herself in her bedroom, not wanting to come out to him, for she knows that will mean change:

> She sat on the bed and drew up her knees tightly against her chest.
> Pressing her head against her knees, she rocked herself. Why did he have to
> come to her? She had come to accept things the way they were. She had been
> getting by. . . .[8]

It is possible to appear godly to others even though our hearts are unchanged. We are still clinging to our sin, to our false idols. We are getting by, though we do not have that inextinguishable joy that comes from enjoying a clear conscience before God.

God is on a quest for our love, for our abandonment to Him, because He knows it is for our best. When we cling to our old ways, He continues to deal with us. It is fascinating to see this in the lives of both Rachel and Jacob and to see how each responded to God's discipline.

Review your memory verse.

18. What is the difference between repentance and remorse? Why do we often choose remorse? Why is this foolish?

_____

_____

19. Read these highlights from Jacob's flight from his Uncle Laban's home:

   A. Genesis 31:1–7
      Despite the fact that he still has a long way to go, there is evidence of spiritual growth in Jacob. Find it in the above passage.

      _____

      _____

   B. Genesis 31:19
      What did Rachel do, and why?

      _____

      _____

   C. Genesis 31:22–35
      What evidence do you find that God is still with Jacob? (v. 24)

      _____

      _____

      What humor can you find in the speech of Laban? How does he get to his main concern at the end of his speech? (vv. 26–30)

      _____

      _____

      What excuse does Rachel use to avoid being searched?

      _____

      _____

      What gods are you hiding under your skirts?

      _____

      _____

Though God dealt with Rachel, she never seemed to come to the point of true repentance and surrender. Though she cried out to Him for help with her infertility, she clung to her father's gods, bickered with her sister all her life, and died in childbirth,

> Without knowing fully what we are doing, we hide the things we secretly love and admire under our skirts, like Rachel, sitting primly and righteously on our camels, wondering why we are not whole, why we still suffer, why we feel unreconciled to the God we profess.[9]
>
> —Leslie Williams

naming her son "son of my misery" (Genesis 35:18). We cannot judge whether she was saved or not, but we can see that she never experienced the lasting joy and peace that accompanies abandonment to the Lord.

Jacob Wrestling with the Angel
GUSTAV DORE (1833–1883)[xi]

∾

Though they have wrestled all night, reflect on the tireless strength this artist portrays in the angel. What a message concerning the futility of resisting God!

D. Genesis 32
What circumstances bring Jacob to the point of terror? (vv. 1–8)

_____

_____

What does Jacob do? How can you see a growing reverence for God? (vv. 9–12)

_____

_____

What evidence do you see that Jacob is still not trusting in God but using carnal weapons? (vv. 13–21)

_____

_____

Describe the wrestling match that took place that night and some of the changes that God made in Jacob's life. (vv. 22–31)

_____

_____

_____

What significance do you see in the name change to *Israel* (meaning "God will rule")?

_____

_____

When Billy and Ruth Graham's son Franklin was a prodigal, Ruth wrote the following prayer:

> O God of Jacob,
> Who knew how to change supplanters then
> Now deal I pray with this my son
> Though he may limp
> When Thou art done.[10]

E. Genesis 33:1–4

What evidence do you see of a repentant Jacob?

_____

_____

What evidence of genuine joy and peace?

_____

_____

Though this was a huge turning point for Jacob, he had not arrived. Shortly after this spiritual victory we see another great failure, in regard to the situation with his daughter, Dinah. Perhaps the lesson is never coast, even after spiritual victory. We must continue to be diligent, to guard our hearts.

Finale

REVIEW

20. Each woman can share, if she chooses, one thing that God impressed on her heart from this study, one way she was "kissed by the King."

PRAYER

How we need each other's help in overcoming sin in our lives! In today's prayer time, it is vital that you determine to keep confidences. Get in circles of three and have each woman name a sin that easily entangles her. Then her sisters should pray for her, that she will have the faith to abandon it and truly repent and go a new direction. Determine to keep praying for the sisters in your small group throughout the week.

You Can't Hurry Love

Prelude

"Dee, have I ever told you the story about my dancing with Jesus . . . *and* he was wearing a tuxedo?"

She never stops surprising me. "I think I would remember," I said, dryly.

She laughed her hearty belly laugh. "I think you would."

And then Kathy told me the most amazing story. I believe God gave her this vision in her first-love time because He knew the dark waters that lay ahead. He wanted to give her the courage to cross those swirling waters triumphantly.

This is the story Kathy told me:

I was going to this little church on Long Island. At a Sunday service during worship, I had my hands up. I was in that abandoned state of praise, that glorious state when God's presence is so near and you can almost touch the boundaries of heaven. All of a sudden a picture came into my head. There I was with Jesus. His strong left hand was in mine and His right hand was on the small of my back. He was gently leading me in a waltz. I couldn't see His face, but He was so manly, elegant, and strong—and He was wearing a tuxedo. I stood there and gazed at us as if I were watching a movie. I couldn't help but think, *Isn't this odd?* My eyes filled with tears as I continued to sing His praises.

A week later I was at our church retreat. They had a couple of guest speakers, and on one particular night, after a time of worship, a prayer line formed. I had a sense of expectation as I waited—I was ready to hear anything God wanted to say to me. When it was my turn, I knelt down, and the speaker's prayers for me were like spring water to my parched soul. Then she said, "I'm trying to get a handle on what I'm seeing . . . you're dancing with Jesus . . . and . . . He has a tuxedo on!" I thought, *This is unbelievable. It's the same vision I had last week.* She continued to describe what she was seeing: "You're in a gigantic ballroom and at the edge of the dance floor are principalities and powers. Jesus is parading you around every corner, saying, 'This is my trophy.'"

I stayed on my knees, weeping.

I was overwhelmed as I realized, *How amazing that God would choose to reveal Himself to me in that way, knowing that romance is so much a part of how I filter the hap-*

penings of life. Here I was thinking it was just me and my craziness—but then, to have this lady say, "Forgive me, but . . ."

What happened to Kathy paints a vivid picture. As believers, Jesus takes our hand and guides us through this earthly journey, while all around us are the forces of darkness. They may taunt us, snicker at us, and rise up in a chorus of condemnation—but all the while Almighty God looks into their faces and says, "Say what you will. She is My Beloved."

This world *is* hard, and we shouldn't be surprised by trials. We *will* suffer. Sometimes, as in the case of Jacob, it is because God, the Master Potter, is refining sin from our lives. Other times, it is not because of sin, but because He has a plan we cannot see. He wants us to trust Him even when He is not making sense. He wants us to trust Him even when He does not immediately deliver us. He wants us to follow Him down the dark and winding path. He is our Shepherd-Prince who will take our hand and lead us to the land of invincible love.

WATCH VIDEO #7: YOU CAN'T HURRY LOVE
Dee will be teaching from John 11.

OPTIONAL NOTE-TAKING SPACE

_____

_____

_____

GROUP RESPONSE TO THE VIDEO
A. What lessons can we learn from Martha in the wilderness?
B. What lessons can we learn from Mary in the wilderness?
C. How might you apply this teaching to your life?

DAY 1

Savior, Like a Shepherd Lead Us

As a young believer, I (Kathy) began to work with a very successful and wealthy manager in New York. My whole family, especially my mother, was so excited that he wanted to work with me. He was a good man, and he believed wholeheartedly in my talent. I worked with him for about a year and got very close to his family.

During this time a producer we were working with had found a song that he and my manager were absolutely convinced was a hit. This was when dance music was so popular. The song was called "Too Bad We're Only Dancing." When I heard the suggestive lyrics, my heart sank because I knew I couldn't sing the song. I knew Jesus by then, and I knew it would be wrong to sing it.

Over the next year I found myself engaged in a full-scale war over this song. At first I asked if we could change the lyrics a little bit. Although the writer wasn't too happy about it, she tried to appease me. But nobody was happy with the revised lyrics. I kept thinking, *Surely we can find another song.* But as wonderful as my manager could be at that time, he was also passionately insistent, and his opinion was dominating the whole situation. By now, record executives were involved, a lot of money was involved, and I was going to get the kind of advance that I'd always dreamed of. The pressure was enormous. Everybody, except one or two friends, thought I was crazy. My mother was so upset. She said, "Kath, your manager loves you. He cares for you. And besides, this is what you've been waiting for!" It was such an emotional time for me. I was crying for days on end, writing in my journal, and wondering how to get out of it. In my gut the Holy Spirit was telling me that I couldn't sing that song. It was black and white to me. But to everyone else it was a gray issue. "What's the big deal?" they would say. But it was totally black and white for me. I kept asking God to do a miracle: "Change my manager's heart! Have another hit song come my way. Oh Lord, I know you can do a parting-of-the-Red-Sea kind of thing."

And yet I kept on hearing *that* voice. "Yes, Kathy, I can. But I want *you* to speak up for what you know is my heart's desire and the right thing to do." It wasn't what I wanted to hear, but I knew that before the Red Sea would part, I had to step into the water.

One of my close friends suggested I go and spend a few days at a retreat center that was just a few hours away. While I was there I was introduced to a Slovakian priest named Father George Torak. What a gentle, humble soul he was. He had been imprisoned for his faith years ago. I admired him very much, for he knew about the forces of darkness, about suffering for Jesus, and about having to make a choice for Him. I am in no way comparing my situation to his, but what a light he was in my darkness. God knew I needed to encounter a man with this kind of conviction. A few days into my fast, I heard a knock at the door. It was Father George. He was so concerned about me and had been praying for me. I invited him in and began to tell him the whole story. Tears came to his eyes as he saw how distraught I was.

I held my head in my hands and said, "I know I have to make a phone call. I have to do this. I know I do. I can't believe all of this turmoil is around one song—but it is. How can I tell my manager that I won't sing it? I know all hell will break loose."

The priest looked at me with such tenderness. Then he patted my hand and said, in his thick Slovakian accent, "With Christ, Kathy, you can do it." He paused. "Do you have anything in your house that you treasure that reminds you of Jesus?"

I didn't quite understand what he was getting at. But in an instant I thought of a picture I had in my bedroom. It had become such a source of comfort to me every time I looked at it. Jesus is holding a lamb close to His face and the lamb's face is kind of squished. It's funny—sometimes people would say, "Really, you like that?"

Interrupting my thoughts, Father George said, "That's perfect, Kathy. I want you to have that close to you as you make the phone call." Then, much to my surprise, that dear priest practiced with me, over and over again, pretending to take the role of my manager. He said, "Keep your eyes on Jesus. You are that little lamb, and He is holding you. Remember who you are, Kathy. Okay, let's try it."

I was trembling, even though it was just make-believe. I realized how much fear I had, and I felt ashamed at how I had allowed myself to become so controlled. Then I pretended to talk into the phone, beginning with, "You know how I've struggled with this song over the last year, and I don't want to hurt you, but I can't do this song."

Then Father George pretended to rant and rave on the other end, saying mock expletives. He said, "I can't believe you are doing this to me, Kathy, after all I've done for you, after the way I've cared for you . . ."

I started to cry and I said, "I *know* you've cared for me, I *know*—"

"No, no, *no*, Kathy!" Father George interrupted me. Then, gently, he said, "Just repeat, 'I cannot do the song.'"

And so I said, "I cannot do the song."

And then he ranted and raved again and I started to apologize again. Firmly he repeated, "No, no, no, Kathy! All you say is, 'I cannot do the song.'" I began to realize that he didn't want me to get caught in the web of manipulation and guilt.

Finally, with a sigh of resignation, I said, "I cannot do the song."

The wise priest smiled. "Now you are ready, Kathy."

Review the following memory verse:

> The LORD your God is with you,
>   he is mighty to save.
> He will take great delight in you,
>   he will quiet you with his love,
>   he will rejoice over you with singing. (Zephaniah 3:17)

1. Describe the test Kathy faced early in her ministry. How do you think her life would have turned out if she had chosen the path her manager wanted her to take?

_____

_____

2. How did God shepherd Kathy through this particular trial?

_____

_____

3. How did God, like the Chief Shepherd in *Hinds' Feet in High Places*, lead Kathy yet not carry her? What choices did she have to make?

_____

_____

4. In your life, give an example of a difficult road the Lord is leading you down. You wish He would just carry you, miraculously deliver you! Yet instead He is prompting you to be disciplined, to make some hard choices—though He promises to be with you.

_____

_____

5. Read John 10:1–6.

A. What picture does Jesus paint? Who is the watchman? The shepherd? The sheep? The stranger?

_____

_____

B. What are some ways you can hear the voice of Jesus? How can you discern His voice from that of a stranger?

_____

_____

C. How did Kathy know, for example, that Jesus was speaking through Father George but not through her manager?

_____

_____

6. Read John 10:7–11.

A. What will happen to you if you follow the Good Shepherd? If you follow the thief?

_____

_____

B. Contrast the heart of the Good Shepherd for you with the heart of the hired man.

_____

_____

7. Read John 10:14–18. How can we be sure of the love of the Good Shepherd, even when His ways are mysterious in our lives?

_____

_____

8. What does it mean to you that Jesus says He is your shepherd and that He knows you, loves you, and will lay down His life for you?

_____

_____

Raindrops Keep Falling on My Head

Often we think that if we choose the right path, things will go well and we will be spared trouble. But actually, we should not be surprised if following in the steps of Jesus leads to persecution and trials. Peter writes:

> Dear friends, do not be surprised at the painful trial you are suffering, as though something strange were happening to you. But rejoice that you participate in the sufferings of Christ, so that you may be overjoyed when his glory is revealed. (1 Peter 4:12–13)

The day came when I (Kathy) made the real phone call to my manager, telling him I could not do the song. It happened just as Father George had predicted. When my manager realized I was standing firm and I was not going to be moved, his anger grew so hot that his words became like fiery darts attacking my soul. Finally, he said, "You'll never, ever hear from me again."

I haven't. It still breaks my heart.

Everybody was so upset with me. I remember going to a friend's house in a kind of a daze. I felt so weary. I knew I needed a safe place where I could remain quiet and catch my breath until the thick black cloud of smoke blew over.

Although it was extremely painful for me, it was one of those times in my life when I was convinced I had done what was pleasing to the Lord. The minute I did what God asked, a weight lifted from me. That didn't mean I wouldn't have consequences to face. Sometimes, when we do what is right, God snatches us out of the wilderness immediately. But more often than not, it takes time. He gives us strength and courage in the battle. He gives us grace and mercy in the suffering. It is true. And the night is darkest just before the dawn.

I was gossiped about. I was slandered. I had to claim bankruptcy to get out of my contract. My mother, who was a widow and wasn't making a lot of money, tried her best to help me out financially. I felt so badly about the loss of relationship with my manager—not just because of what it meant for my career, but also because I truly cared about him and his family. I still pray about that relationship to this day.

I started singing at weddings and funerals for forty dollars a pop. Often people would come up to me and say, "Honey, did you ever think about doing this professionally?" It was so humbling for me because I had traveled the country and made records, and here I was standing in a balcony somewhere singing "Sunrise, Sunset."

I think the lesson of the Book of Job is "Will you trust God even when there is no immediate reward?" If He does take us out of the wilderness immediately, when does our faith have a chance to grow? It's in the wilderness that we learn to surrender, where we learn to really say, "My life is in Your hands. My heart is in Your keeping."

I think that's what happened to Mary and Martha of Bethany. I believe it was in the desperate hours when their faith really grew. They expected Jesus to come running when Lazarus became ill. They sent Him a message: "Lord, the one you love is sick" (John 11:3b).

But Jesus didn't come running. He stayed where He was. And Lazarus died. How abandoned they must have felt.

Begin learning this verse:

> Even though I walk
>> through the valley of the shadow of death,
> I will fear no evil,
>> for you are with me;
> Your rod and your staff,
>> they comfort me. (Psalm 23:4)

9. As a believer, when you are trying to live for the Lord, are you surprised by suffering? What should be your reaction?

_____

_____

Today we will continue studying the context that leads to the incident in which we find Mary and Martha of Bethany in the wilderness. Jesus' life on earth is drawing to a close. He is in Jerusalem, less that two miles away from Bethany. He has just explained that He is the good shepherd and that He is going to lay down His life for the sheep. Note how hostile the questioning is, and how steadfast is our Lord.

10. Read John 10:19–42.

A. Describe the growing division and hostility concerning Jesus. (vv. 19–21)

_____

_____

B. What do the Jerusalem Jews demand? (v. 24)

_____

C. How does Jesus answer them? (vv. 25–30)

_____

_____

D. What is their reaction? (v. 31)

_____

E. What accusation do they make against Jesus? (v. 33)

_____

_____

It is vital to realize that Jesus claimed to be God. This is why they crucified Him. C. S. Lewis has said that this cuts away the middle ground that many try to stand on, saying that Jesus was simply a good teacher. They will therefore consider His words but not give Him their lives.

F. What does Jesus tell them they should take note of? (vv. 37–38)

_____

G. Where does Jesus go? (v. 40)

_____

This was a full day's journey from Bethany.

11. Read John 11:1–5. Does your knowledge of the preceding chapter give you any insights into this passage? If so, what?

_____

_____

12. Job tells us we see "only the edges of His ways" (Job 26:14 NKJV). If there is an area in your life that is very painful to you right now, what do you know about Jesus and His miracles that could help you to trust Him?

_____

_____

> You must make your choice. Either this man was, and is, the Son of God: or else a madman or something worse. You can shut Him up for a fool, you can spit at Him and kill Him as a demon; or you can fall at His feet and call Him Lord and God. But let us not come with any patronising nonsense about His being a great human teacher. He has not left that open to us. He did not intend to.[3]
>
> —C. S. Lewis

Send in the Clowns

This little family in Bethany was one of the few healthy families in Scripture. They seemed to have no father or mother living with them, but the three siblings were a beautiful family unit. Though there were times of tension, their love for one another was strong and deep. They also had a dear friend in Jesus, who became a source of strength for them. They'd heard about His miracles, perhaps had even witnessed them firsthand, and they had listened carefully to His words. They trusted Him implicitly, and they were confident of His heart for them.

Therefore, when Lazarus became ill, the sisters huddled together. What should they do? They knew it might be dangerous for Jesus to come to Bethany, because when He was in nearby Jerusalem, a short time ago, the Jews tried to stone Him. Yet, *still*, they knew He would come. After all, He loved them. And they had cared for Him so often. There had been times when Martha had fixed a whole banquet for Him and all of His disciples, providing an incredible feast of meats, breads, and sweets that lit up their eyes and satisfied their appetites. And when Jesus came alone, Martha had always eagerly washed His feet and prepared a special meal, just for Him. She had served Him—now, surely, in her hour of need, He would serve her. And so, the sisters whispered together and agreed. They would send word:

Lord, the one you love is sick. (John 11:3b)

What is Jesus' response to the messenger? It is good news—news to cheer an anxious heart:

This sickness will not end in death. No, it is for God's glory so that God's
Son may be glorified through it. (John 11:4)

As they sponged their dear brother's feverish brow, they must have thought, *The Master will come. He will touch Lazarus, speak a word—and his fever will disappear, his pain will be gone.* "Hang on, dear Lazarus," they must have said. "We will laugh and eat together again."

However, Jesus *didn't* come instantly. The following two verses, juxtaposed, seem like a contradiction:

Jesus loved Martha and her sister and Lazarus. Yet when he heard that
Lazarus was sick, he stayed where he was two more days. (John 11:5–6)

The clouds slowly roll in. The storm is imminent. *Where is He?* Can't you picture the sisters continually glancing out the window, expecting to see Jesus striding purposely up the path? Martha is trying all kinds of medicinal herbs, spooning broth into her brother's mouth. All the while anger must have been growing in her heart. *Jesus! All You would have to do is speak the word—and Lazarus would be well. Why are You taking so long? You know that with every hour that passes by his body grows weaker and his spirit even more. Don't You care?*

And can't you picture Mary consoling Lazarus, saying, "The Master will come any moment, Lazarus. Remember His kind heart, my brother. Though He may tarry, He *will* come! I know He will."

But where is Jesus?

Lazarus dies, and quickly his body grows cold. How devastated the sisters were. How could Jesus let this happen? Is this love? How could He let them down like this? Because they were a prominent family, many, many Jews came to mourn with them, but some of their visitors wondered:

> Could not he who opened the eyes of the blind man have kept this man
> from dying? (John 11:37)

When Jesus finally *does come*, after Lazarus has been dead for four days, each sister says exactly the same thing to Jesus: "Lord, if you had been here, my brother would not have died." They expected Him to deliver them. And He didn't.

Charles Spurgeon says:

> He does not say: "I regret that I have tarried so long." He does not say, "I
> ought to have hastened, but even now it is not too late." Hear and marvel!
> Wonder of wonders, he says, "I am *glad* that I was not there! **Glad!** . . .
> Martha and Mary are weeping their eyes out for sorrow, and yet their friend
> Jesus is glad!⁴

Is this love? Like high-flying trapeze artists they reached for the hand they absolutely expected to be there, the hand that should have rescued them. But to their amazement, to their horror, He is not there.

13. What stood out to you from today's introduction? Why?

_____

_____

To prepare your heart, review your memory verse and read all of John 11 as an overview.

14. What stood out to you from this overview reading? Why?

_____

_____

15. How might some see John 11:5 as contradicting John 11:6? Comment.

_____

_____

God allows us to be in the wilderness—in fact, sometimes He is _glad_ to put us in the wilderness—so that our faith will grow. We're so fickle. Often, we don't hang onto Him when everything is bright and prosperous. After I (Kathy) said no to the song "Too Bad We're Only Dancing," I went through one of the hardest times of my life. But I believe Jesus was _glad,_ for I learned to meet Him with more abandon. I had nothing to go on but His Word. All I knew was that God was somehow going to continue to guide me and provide the grace I needed during this time. I didn't know what I was going to encounter around the corner, but I knew Who was going with me.

Yes, it was in the wilderness that I experienced all sorts of tumultuous emotions. But I also came to know His comfort, His faithfulness, and His love in a whole new way. And today, looking back, I see that choosing the easy way out may have spared me initial suffering, and even caused a false peace, but I would surely have been headed toward a slow death. Choosing the high road may take me through my deepest pain, but I will always come out where God dwells—a place of beauty, a place where life can flourish, and a place where my heart can be at peace.

16. Share a wilderness experience during which your faith grew and you experienced His comfort, His faithfulness, and His love in a whole new way.

_____

_____

_____

Review Week 4's memory verses, thinking of them in terms of following Jesus even when He doesn't make sense, even when His path leads to the cross:

> _Entreat me not to leave thee, or to return from following after thee: for whither thou goest, I will go; and where thou lodgest, I will lodge: thy people shall be my people, and thy God my God:_
> _Where thou diest, will I die, and there will I be buried: the LORD do so to me, and more also, if ought but death part thee and me._ (Ruth 1:16–17 KJV)

What Now My Love?

When I (Dee) read Kathy's journal entries to the man she prays will one day be her husband, I see the ache. The questioning. The wondering. *Why is God taking so long?*

> *October 26, 1997*
>
> *You seem like some far away dream today . . . a fairy tale that only happens for other people . . .*
>
> *Been feeling hopeless and deeply saddened by my feelings or lack of them . . . It seems that I go in seasons or cycles of hope to an almost despair . . . I could sob . . .*
>
> *March 20, 1998*
>
> *On the road . . . Thinking about turning forty a lot lately. Wondering if you'll always be a sweet dream of mine*
>
> *The years are passing so fast . . .*
>
> *Will I ever read this to you . . . ? Or are my writings in vain . . . ?*

Surely a similar impatience and frustration was felt by Mary and Martha of Bethany as they waited for Jesus to come and heal their brother. And then, when Lazarus died, their hearts were sick, for "hope deferred makes the heart sick" (Proverbs 13:12).

How did they feel when Jesus appeared after their brother had been in the grave for four days?

We don't have to guess. Martha is the first to confront Jesus, and she is quite clear about her feelings.

We can learn something very important from Martha. When we are in the wilderness, it is vital that we keep dialoguing with the Lord. Just as in a marriage, when there is trouble, it is important that we keep talking, speaking the truth in love, and that we keep listening, allowing our heart to be teachable.

So it is in our love relationship with Jesus. And Martha shows us the way.

Review this week's memory verse:

> *Even though I walk*
> > *through the valley of the shadow of death,*
> *I will fear no evil,*
> > *for you are with me;*
> *Your rod and your staff,*
> > *they comfort me.* (Psalm 23:4)

17. Read John 11:17–27.

    A. Describe the scene in verses 17–20.

    _____

    _____

    B. What does Martha say to Jesus? (vv. 21–22) What admirable qualities do you see in her?

    _____

    _____

    C. How does Jesus respond to her? (v. 23)

    _____

    D. What does she think He means? How do you think she feels? (v. 24)

    _____

    _____

    E. What statement does Jesus then make? And what question does He ask of Martha? (v. 25)

    _____

    _____

Some disappointment is revealed in this speech, such as we have all felt with the promise of an ultimate resurrection, when the grave has closed over some dear friend. We find small relief in the assurance. The old ties are snapped, the old ways are at an end.[5]

—H. R. Reynolds

The question Jesus asked Martha reminds me of the question He asked me (Kathy) when my mother was dying. He asked me, *Am I not still God?* It was hard for me to respond, but I knew I must. I believe it was hard for Martha to respond, but she did, and she did it with faith and strength. At a time when she was in great pain, she acknowledged that Jesus was Lord, that He was in control, and that He was who He claimed to be.

    F. Describe Martha's answer. (v. 27)

    _____

    G. What does she then do that substantiates her answer? (v. 28)

    _____

18. In this week's memory verse, we see that "your rod and your staff comfort me." The rod was a symbol of God's sovereignty. How can the truth of God's sovereignty and control comfort you in the wilderness? How do you think it comforted Martha?

_____

_____

19. Read John 11:28–37.

    A. Describe how Mary responds to her sister's news. What does this tell you?

    _____

    _____

    B. What does Mary do when she reaches Jesus, and what does she say? Describe her emotion. (vv. 32-33)

    _____

    _____

    C. Describe the response of Jesus to her tears and to the tears of the others. (v. 35) What does this tell you?

    _____

    _____

Did Jesus weep because the situation was out of His control? Did He weep because He made a mistake in tarrying? No. We believe He wept because Mary and others were weeping and He loved them so. He knew they didn't understand and that they couldn't see into the future. Though He allows us to go through the wilderness so that our faith will grow, He still grieves for the pain we feel. He sees our tears and He cares. I (Kathy) love the verse that says:

> You have collected all my tears and preserved them in your bottle! (Psalm 56:8b TLB)

How intimate of God to be aware of my tears. Not one of them is casually discarded by Him.

20. The "staff" was a symbol of comfort, for the shepherd would reach down with his staff and lift the sheep from dangers, such as being out on a precipice or caught in a rushing stream. How did Jesus comfort Mary in the wilderness? How has He comforted you?

    _____

    _____

21. Are you facing a wilderness experience right now? What can you learn from Jesus' encounter with Martha or with Mary that might be of help to you?

    _____

    _____

Faith begins in the wilderness—when you are alone and afraid, when things don't make sense . . . . In the wilderness of loneliness we are terribly vulnerable. . . . But we may be missing the fact that it is here . . . here where we may learn to love Him—here where it seems He is not at work, where His will seems obscure or frightening, where He is not doing what we expected Him to do. . . . If faith does not go to work here it will not go to work at all.

God's answer is always: "trust me."[6]

—*Elisabeth Elliot*

DAY 5

I Hear a Symphony

I (Dee) have often felt, as I know many people have, that being single is second best despite Scripture's clear stand that it is good to remain single, if you can, because you can be fully devoted to the Lord (1 Corinthians 7:25–35). I have been a matchmaker, as I wanted my dear women friends to know the joy of marriage and motherhood. The single life, despite what Scripture has to say, is not what I've wanted for them.

Yet getting to know Kathy, and seeing what the single life has birthed in her, has caused me to reassess. Though marriage and motherhood are great, great blessings, a single woman, if she remains open to God in her singleness, can have a ministry and an intimacy with the Lord that we who are married may never know. And in the eternal scheme of things, is that not what is most important? I *truly* believe that if God brings you a man, a good man, you should rejoice. What a wonderful gift. But if He does not, there is also reason to rejoice. Life is not about a wife or a husband; it is about a love affair with God. In that you will always be fulfilled.

I believe Kathy provides a wonderful model, not only to single women, but to all of us. We all have longings, though they are different for each of us. We may long for a husband—or a changed husband! We may long to be used in a successful ministry. We may pine for a healthy body, a healed relationship, or even a bigger house. We should ask God for those things, remembering He is smarter than we are and may say "Not now." While we are waiting and wondering if He will ever say "Yes," how should we deal with those unfulfilled longings? Kathy models a marvelous perspective for us. Her dear friend Allyson put it like this:

> Kath's struck a wonderful balance. She's not so needy that she feels incomplete without a spouse; she's not looking around every corner for a man. But neither is she at the other end of the pendulum: without hope, dead, and shut down. She is standing in the middle place, which says: God may never send a mate, but I sure hope He does. There's an ache and a thrill in that, and she embraces them both.

We also need to deal with the fundamental question of motive. Why do we want the things we want? Is our motive one that is truly pleasing to God? Kathy has come to terms with that as well, as reflected in one of her later journal entries:

August 7, 1999

> *There were times in my life when I yearned for you and wanted you for certain reasons. Just the sheer expectation of my reaching a cer-*

tain age—and I'd be married—have a house, have security, possibly
children. I'd imagine many different scenarios of romance and tender
moments. Besides—I pride myself on being so alive to give and receive
in a passionate relationship. I've had to watch other people for so
long—getting to share that with one another.

Time, age—maturity—the process of life—has brought me to a place of
wanting you for far different reasons. Possibly even one.

I want to be holy. I want to be God's woman. If you coming into my
life will give me more of that . . . more of Jesus, then I say, "Yes, Lord.
Please bring him to me."

Will Kathy ever marry? I don't know. Often I cannot see how she could be used, the amazing way she is being used, if she also had to focus on pleasing a husband. But then I am reminded that we belong to a God who can do anything. He could, if He chose, give Kathy a man who was *so* godly that he would not be threatened at all by her success and would long to give her the support she needs for her ministry and her endless days on the road.

Just when Martha had resigned herself that she would not see Lazarus until heaven, Jesus absolutely astonished her. Her brother had been dead for four days and she was convinced all was over. Even that waiting period, in retrospect, was completely in His plan. Martha and Mary learned important lessons in that waiting time. The scene was also completely set for the most dramatic of events. Why? The Jews believed that the soul hovered around the body for three days to make sure it was really dead. But when the body began to decay, the soul fled. After three days in the grave, the Jews knew all was over.

Their only hope now was a miracle.

22. Tell Jesus about a longing of your heart. Then put it in His hands.

_____

_____

23. Read John 11:38–44.

A. What does Jesus ask, and how does Martha dialogue with Him about her concerns? (vv. 38–39)

_____

_____

B. How does Jesus respond to Martha's concern? (v. 40)

_____

_____

C. If you read between the lines of verses 40 and 41, Martha must have given a nod of her head to the men. She was the mistress of the house, and they were looking to her. This evidences a teachable heart. How have you seen this in other ways concerning Martha?

_____

_____

D. What have you learned from Martha about dialoguing with the Lord?

_____

_____

E. What does Jesus say in His prayer? (vv. 41–42)

_____

_____

F. Describe the miracle. (vv. 43–44) Using your imagination, describe the sisters.

_____

_____

The Raising of Lazarus
SALVATOR ROSA (1615–1673)[xii]

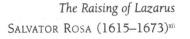

The artist has captured the authority of Christ, the stir among the people, and the profound emotions of Martha and Mary.

24. Describe the response to the raising of Lazarus in the following passages:

    A. John 11:45 _____

    B. John 11:47–48 _____

    C. John 11:53 and 12:10–11 _____

    _____

25. Scripture is clear that unbelief is not due to a lack of knowledge, or even under-standing. It is not a head problem, but a heart problem (see Romans 10:9–21). How is this evidenced here by the response of some to the raising of Lazarus?

    _____

    _____

In the same way, our lack of obedience to the Lord is not a head problem. We know the right way. It is a heart problem. We must daily pray that we would fall more deeply in love with Jesus.

Finale

REVIEW

26. Each woman can share, if she chooses, one thing that God impressed on her heart from this study, one way she was "kissed by the King."

PRAYER

Read your answer to either question 4 or question 21. Allow your sisters to support you with sentence prayers. Then support them as they read their answers.

ACT III

Invincible Love

⁀⁀

Orchestra
tranquillo risoluto
(Play peacefully but with passionate confidence)

Unforgettable

Prelude

When Cinderella appeared at the ball, the whispering began: "Who is this gracious and beautiful woman?"

When Eliza Doolittle (played by Audrey Hepburn in the movie version of *My Fair Lady*) made her entrance, every head turned. "How lovely!" "How enchanting!" "She must be a princess!"

These women had been transformed—one by a fairy godmother, another by a professor skilled in language and social graces. Their appearance startled people, people stared, and the whispering began. "Who could this be? Why have we missed her? She is so beautiful."

Bonnie Raitt sings "Something to Talk About." Suppose Jesus said to you, "Let's give them something to talk about!" Imagine if when you left a room full of people they'd be saying, "Isn't she interesting? Isn't she lovely? She loves God in a way I haven't seen." Wouldn't it be wonderful if people would consider the reality of Christ after being with you? When we are honest, we admit that we want people to think that we are radiant, that we are women of substance and depth. But what really matters is that we be godly women, women who possess so much of Jesus that people believe He exists because He is so powerful in us. We should leave behind the fragrance of Christ, a fragrance that stays on their mind.

Mary of Bethany certainly did that. When she left the party she attended nearly two thousand years ago, they were talking—and they haven't stopped.

WATCH VIDEO #8: UNFORGETTABLE
Dee will be teaching from John 12.

OPTIONAL NOTE-TAKING SPACE

_____

_____

_____

_____

A. What stood out to you from the anointing of Jesus by Mary of Bethany?
B. In the story Dee told, what were some things in her alabaster box?
C. What is in your alabaster box?
D. How might you apply this teaching to your life?

DAY 1

Something to Talk About

The remarkable event with Mary of Bethany occurred shortly after the raising of Lazarus and just days before the crucifixion of Christ. It occurred at a party thrown by a man known as Simon the Leper. He had obviously been healed of his leprosy and had been restored to the community. He was extremely grateful, not only for his own restoration, but now also for the restoration of Lazarus. Therefore he held a dinner in Jesus' honor. The party was already extraordinary, with Jesus as the guest of honor and with Lazarus, a man who had been buried for four days, reclining at the table with Jesus. Martha is busy serving, but Mary, at first, is nowhere to be seen.

And then, she appears at the door. She is carrying her alabaster jar. Women of marrying age had a jar or a box made of alabaster, which was a kind of marble. In it was a precious fragrance, and the container was sealed to protect it. Mary's container apparently had a long and slender neck that could be easily broken. In their book, *Lady in Waiting*, Debby Jones and Jackie Kendall explain the significance of this possession:

> In the days Jesus was on earth, when a young woman reached the age of availability for marriage, her family would purchase an alabaster box for her and fill it with precious ointment. The size of the box and the value of the ointment would parallel her family's wealth. This alabaster box would be part of her dowry. When a young man came to ask for her in marriage, she would respond by taking the alabaster box and breaking it at his feet. This gesture of anointing his feet showed him honor.[1]

That day, I imagine all eyes went to Mary when she appeared. Did the guests whisper? "What is she doing?" "Why does she have her alabaster bottle?" And then they watched in amazement as she did what she absolutely had to do.

> *Then Mary took about a pint of pure nard, an expensive perfume; she poured it on Jesus' feet and wiped his feet with her hair. And the house was filled with the fragrance of the perfume.* (John 12:3)

Mary's perfume was very valuable indeed. It was worth approximately one year's wages. But rather than saving it for her earthly bridegroom, she chose to break the bottle, or perhaps the seal on the bottle, and anoint Jesus. First, according to Mark and Matthew, she poured some on His head. Then, according to John, she sank to her knees and poured the rest on His feet, wiping them with her long and flowing hair. Perhaps she used her hair, rather than a towel, as an indication of her great love for Jesus. Leon Morris writes:

> The act is all the more striking in that a Jewish lady never unbound her hair in public. That apparently was a mark of loose morals. But Mary did not stop to calculate public reaction. Her heart went out to her Lord and she gave expression to something of her feelings in this beautiful and touching act.[2]

A woman's alabaster bottle was her most precious possession. Mary of Bethany loved Jesus so—and now He was also her Prince who had rescued her by raising her brother from the dead. A. B. Bruce writes:

> She loved Jesus with her whole heart, for what He was, for what He had done for the family . . . there was such love in her heart . . . yet it could not find expression in words. She must do something to relieve her pent-up emotions: she must get her alabaster box and break it, and pour it on the person of Jesus, else her heart will break.[3]

The risk she took was astonishing. Women were supposed to stay in the background. Yet here, with one overwhelming intention, Mary of Bethany boldly enters a house full of men. It doesn't matter to her that she is risking her pride, her reputation, and her dowry—she is ready to abandon all for Jesus. What she does is dramatic, and it causes an enormous stir. The perfume's fragrance filled the whole house and lingered, no doubt, on Jesus through the following holy week, through His crucifixion, and on His body in the grave. She certainly gave them something to talk about.

Begin memorizing:

> *I have been crucified with Christ and I no longer live, but Christ lives in me. The life I live in the body, I live by faith in the Son of God, who loved me and gave himself for me. (Galatians 2:20)*

1. Have you ever been so overwhelmed with love for Jesus that you simply had to do something? If so, share something about it.

     _____

     _____

2. What did you learn from this week's Prelude and today's introduction that was significant to you? Why?

_____

_____

_____

This incident involving Mary of Bethany is told by Matthew, Mark, and John. Luke records a similar but different incident, and it is often confused with this one. It is important that you see that these were two different incidents, two different women, two different hosts, and two different lessons. To help clarify this, and also to give you a glimpse of yet another woman who was deeply in love with Jesus, we will look briefly at this incident in Luke.

3. Read Luke 7:36–50.

    A. What are the name and the description given of the host of this party? (vv. 39–40)

        _____

    B. What can you discern about the host's character? Give verse references.

        _____

        _____

In Luke, the host was Simon the Pharisee, and in Matthew, Mark, and John, in the incident with Mary of Bethany, the host was Simon the Leper. Though both hosts were named Simon (Simon was a very common name), these were two different Simons. How do we know? First, a Pharisee could never have been a leper, even a healed leper. Also, Simon the Leper, in the incident with Mary of Bethany, was throwing a party in grateful adoration of Jesus—hardly the motive for the "hospitality" of Simon the Pharisee.

    C. The incident with Mary of Bethany occurred at the end of Jesus' ministry, shortly before He was to be crucified. What evidence can you find that the incident in Luke was closer to the beginning of Jesus' ministry?

        _____

        _____

    D. How is this woman described? (Luke 7:37)

        _____

        _____

The phrase "led a sinful life" implies she had a reputation for some kind of immorality, probably sexual immorality. Some identify the woman as Mary Magdalene, and this error has been widely spread. But that is unlikely. As Darrell Bock explains, Mary Magdalene is named in the next chapter with no mention that she was the woman in this incident.[4] Also, Scripture never says that Mary Magdalene led a life of immorality, though Hollywood films have often portrayed her that way. What we do know is that Mary Magdalene was delivered from seven demons and was absolutely devoted to Jesus (Luke 8:2). Neither was this woman Mary of Bethany, for there is no indication that Mary of Bethany led a life of immorality. However, what this un-named woman had in common with both of these Mary's was a deep love for Jesus, the burning desire to express that love, and the courage to carry it off. Surely she knew the Pharisees who had gathered at Simon's house would be critical of her, but she simply had to express her love to Jesus. Note also how she breaks down and weeps. The word Luke uses for "weeping" is significant, as it is often used to describe rain showers. One of the central themes of the Gospel of Luke is that salvation is open to all, that no matter your past, Jesus can make you clean. This woman, who had been forgiven much, was absolutely overcome with gratitude and love.

E. An intriguing aspect of this story is Jesus' explanation for the sinful woman's great love. What is it? (v. 47) Can you identify with this? If so, explain.

_____

_____

4. Read Matthew's account of the incident involving Mary of Bethany (Matthew 26:9–13). (Only John names her, but it is clear that Matthew and Mark are describing the same incident.) What differences do you note from the incident in Luke that make it clear that this is not the same incident?

_____

_____

DAY 2

Call Me Irresponsible

Mary of Bethany is often criticized. When she sat at the feet of Jesus in her first-love time, her sister became angry, believing that Mary's place was in the kitchen with her. Yet when Martha criticized her, Mary did not jump to her feet and defend herself. Do you remember who did defend Mary?

Jesus. And He did it very well.

A characteristic of someone who is deeply in love with Jesus is that her deepest desire is to please Him, and the longing for the praise of man diminishes. Most people live for the praise of man, so an individual focused on pleasing God becomes quite remarkable. A person like this has such adoration and confidence in the Lord that she believes He will defend her. She follows in the steps of Christ. "When they hurled their insults at him, he did not retaliate; when he suffered, he made no threats. Instead, he entrusted himself to him who judges justly" (1 Peter 2:23).

Was Mary hurt by the criticism she received? We imagine she was, for she was human. But she was so focused on Jesus that she couldn't think about pleasing man. She also repeatedly saw that Jesus came to her rescue with a strong defense.

This time, Mary's action made her the target of criticism from His disciples.

Continue to learn your memory verse.

5. Review Mary in her first-love time (Luke 10:38–42) and note how she was criticized and how she responded. How did Jesus defend her?

_____

_____

6. Read John 12:1–8.

   A. Note the timing of this incident. What has just occurred? (John 11) What is about to occur? (John 12:1 and 12:23–24) What significance do you see in the timing?

   _____

   _____

   B. What is the purpose of the party? (John 12:2)

   _____

   C. Describe what each of the three siblings is doing. (vv. 2–3)

   _____

   D. Who is the first to criticize Mary? What is his motive? (vv. 4–6)

   _____

   E. Who defends Mary? What does He say? (vv. 7–8)

   _____

   _____

7. Read Mark 14:1–9.

   A. Mark shows us that after Judas criticized Mary, the other disciples jumped on the bandwagon. What are their argument and tone? (vv. 4–5)

_____

_____

How easily we are influenced by the opinion of others! In John's Gospel, Judas, with one hand in the moneybag, is criticizing Mary with a lofty-sounding argument about his deep concern for the poor. Now we see, here in Mark, the disciples quickly joining in, harping on poor Mary. Jesus is about to give them a wake-up call. Can you imagine how this must have humbled them? And can you imagine how that feeling intensified weeks later when they clearly saw the whole picture: the death of Jesus, the heart of Judas, and the amazing perception of Mary? How cautious we need to be before we jump to conclusions and criticize others!

B. What is the first statement Jesus makes to them, and what is His first question? (v. 6a)

_____

C. What does Jesus say about the poor? (v. 7) Is He saying we shouldn't be concerned about the poor? Compare this with Deuteronomy 15:11.

_____

_____

_____

D. Note everything Jesus says about Mary. (vv. 6, 8–9)

_____

8. Read Proverbs 16:7 and explain the condition of God being our defender.

_____

_____

Today, make it your goal not to defend yourself (not even once!) but to commit your case to the One who judges justly. Tomorrow, record how you did.

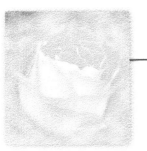

DAY 3

Color My World

My (Kathy's) favorite time of year is autumn. Leaves turning, it's nature's fashion show. Armani, Calvin Klein, and Versace wish they could look this good! Yet what penetrates my heart is that amidst this lavish exhibit, there is a complete dying process going on. Every leaf that boldly expresses its splendor will eventually fall to the ground. Dry and barren. Its beauty seemingly gone forever. Until spring . . . new buds, new life, a new creation.

When we die to ourselves, when we break our alabaster box, it is an act of faith—that from death will come life. Do we believe there will be a resurrection? So often we don't believe it. We don't want to die to ourselves because we don't believe God will do His part. But He will.

He certainly did with Mary of Bethany. When she broke her alabaster bottle, Jesus turned and canonized her on the spot. He praised her, blessed her, and said that what she did would be remembered always. She must have treasured that moment for the rest of her life.

Did Mary really know what she was doing? Jesus said that she poured perfume on Him to prepare His body for burial. Did she know Jesus was going to be crucified? Did she intend for her perfume to anoint Him for His burial? Some are absolutely convinced she understood; others are just as convinced she did not.

Obviously Mary was overwhelmed with love and had to find a way to express it. Perhaps she didn't realize how meaningful her act was going to be. Perhaps she knew He was going to die but didn't know how soon or that she was actually preparing His body for burial. Perhaps Christ's words astonished her as they undoubtedly did the disciples.

I (Kathy) have often been led to do something without knowing exactly why. When we choose to take the hand of Jesus even though we may not know where He's leading, He has a certain destination in mind, and it will be a delightful surprise to our souls.

Several years back when I was in a quaint little town in Austria, I saw a crucifix in the window of a little carpenter's shop. It was exquisitely hand carved: the veins, the agony, the sorrow. It was the most unbelievable cross I'd ever seen. The shop was closed, but some people on the street gestured to the apartment upstairs. I ran up the steps and knocked on the door. A tall man peeked out. Using gestures, I communicated, "Are you the carpenter who owns the shop? Will you open it up? I want the cross in the window." He politely came down, opened the doors, and sold the magnificent cross to me. I knew I would cherish it forever.

On the way home, while I was lifting the package to put it in the overhead on the plane, so excited to have found this awesome piece of art, God suddenly spoke to my spirit. *You need to give this to Breeda.* (Breeda is a dear friend of mine. She prays diligently for me and is one of the godliest women I know.)

"What?" I said. "Breeda? Really? . . . Why?"

You need to give the cross to Breeda.

"Well . . . well . . . okay, Lord. Okay."

Not too long after that, I planned to meet some friends for dinner at an Italian restaurant. Breeda was going to be there. I wrapped up the cross and found myself with a sense of joyful anticipation. When I saw her, I hugged her and said, "I know this is strange, but I have something for you. God told me to give this to you."

She opened it up and tears began to sweetly flow. "You don't know how much I've been praying that God would just show me a sign," she cried, "of how much He loves me." I started weeping too, because although I hadn't realized Breeda's need, God had. He asked me to do something, and I'm so thankful I obeyed. It turned out to be a huge blessing for both of us. I think that's how it might have been for Mary of Bethany. Sometimes we do things out of obedience and only later understand God's purpose.

One of the exciting aspects of this romance with Jesus is that it is a great adventure. As we cultivate listening to His still, small voice, as we have a sense of expectation when we open His Word, and as we move out, in faith, to follow His leading, even when that means following Him to the cross and dying to ourselves, great surprises await us. He will bring light and life to our hearts as absolutely no one else can do.

Prepare your heart by reviewing your memory verse. If you choose, spend some time on your knees in praise, or sing to the Lord.

9. Yesterday, as you practiced not defending yourself but committing your case to Jesus, how did you do?

   _____

   _____

10. In Mark 14:9, how does Jesus canonize Mary on the spot?

    _____

    _____

11. How did Mary's act of abandonment turn out to be a huge blessing, not only for her, but for generations to come?

    _____

    _____

12. Repeatedly God promises us that He will bless us for our obedience, He will surprise us for our acts of faith.

    A. Read Psalm 37:4.
       What promise is given and what is the condition of the promise?

       _____

       _____

As you learn to delight in the Lord, He makes some amazing changes in your heart. Recently a woman at a seminar said to me (Dee), remembering my desire as a young woman to have a house overlooking the Pacific, "So you live in Nebraska! I don't think you could get any farther from the ocean."

I laughed. "I don't think you could."

"But it doesn't matter at all, does it?" She smiled.

I nodded, realizing again how much more God had given me than I ever could have dreamed for myself. Sometimes He gives us the desires of our hearts, but just as often, as we delight in Him, He changes those desires, giving us a yearning for different things, for *His* things.

I (Kathy) have had the same experience. Recently the Lord allowed me to sing on the stage at Dollywood. All of my life I have dreamed of being in a setting like that and singing songs like "Embraceable You." But it's funny—afterwards I thought, *This does not compare to the joy I experience when I sing about Jesus. Seeing lives touched and transformed has affected my heart deeply. God has truly changed my desires.*

> How have you seen Psalm 37:4 fulfilled in your life? How has God been changing your desires?
>
> _____
>
> _____

B. Read Isaiah 58:5–11.
   What promises are given, and what are the conditions of the promises?

   _____

   _____

   _____

   How have you seen the above fulfilled in your life? Think about a time when God strengthened you, when He made you feel like a "well-watered garden."

   _____

   _____

C. Read Matthew 6:28–33.
   What promise is given, and what is the condition of the promise? (v. 33)

   _____

   _____

   If possible, share a time when you have seen the above fulfilled in your life, especially when God surprised you.

   _____

   _____

13. How did Jesus surprise Mary of Bethany in each of her love stages? What did you

Faith is work. It is a struggle. You must struggle with all your heart. . . . And on the way, God will ambush you.[5]

—Walter Wangerin

see in her life that made the conditions ripe for God's exciting "ambush," His startling blessings?

A. First Love (Luke 10:38–42) _____

_____

B. Wilderness Love (John 11)_____

_____

C. Invincible Love (John 12:1–8)_____

_____

DAY 4

I Can See Clearly Now

Perhaps Mary didn't understand that Jesus was going to die very soon and that she was anointing Him for His burial. I (Dee) certainly agree with Kathy that often we have no idea of why we are doing something, but we obey that still, small voice and later can see the dramatic impact of our obedience.

However, I believe Mary of Bethany *did* understand what she was doing. Perhaps it is simply my pride as a woman that relishes the thought that a woman, considered to be the inferior gender in that culture (but not by Jesus), gleaned what all the men had missed. For some time Jesus had been telling His followers that He was going to Jerusalem to die, and they'd look at Him with glazed eyes and say, "Huh?"

But isn't it at least possible that Mary, alone among the disciples, understood? It seems to me that Jesus implied she understood. I have often seen that those who sit at the feet of Jesus, listening to Him intently, are more apt to see things that fly completely over the heads of others. I have also seen that obedience leads to deeper revelations.

Repeatedly in Scripture the Lord lets us know that those who earnestly desire to know Him, to see Him, and to obey Him will understand mysteries that others cannot understand. He spoke in riddles and parables to hide things from those who were not welcoming Him but was eager to reveal Himself to those with seeking hearts. Do you remember how the Lord said, "Shall I hide from Abraham what I am about to do" (Genesis 18:17)? The Lord chose not to hide the truth from Abraham, the friend of God. I think it is possible that the Lord chose also not to hide the truth from Mary of Bethany because she too was truly His friend and earnestly desired to understand and obey. Dallas Willard, in *The Divine Conspiracy*, helps us to understand why some believers are able to see spiritual mysteries and others struggle:

Seeing is no simple thing, of course. Often a great deal of knowledge, experience, imagination, patience, and receptivity is required. . . . But seeing is all the more difficult in spiritual things, where the objects . . . must be willing to be seen.

Persons rarely become present where they are not heartily wanted. Certainly that is true for you and me. We prefer to be wanted, warmly wanted, before we reveal our souls—or even come to a party.

The ability to see and the practice of seeing God and God's world comes through a process of seeking and growing in intimacy with him.[6]

I think it is at least possible that Mary of Bethany grasped that Jesus was on His way to the cross, because she loved Him so much and heartily wanted to understand Him. The psalmist tells us the Lord confides in those who worship Him (based on Psalm 25:14a AMP).

When I read a commentary that says, "Of course Mary didn't understand," I think, *Why do you say "of course"?* Is it because she was a woman? Is it because the others were not grasping the truth?

Mary had seen Jesus raise her brother from the dead. She had seen Him do the impossible. She also could see that not all were pleased. Did she hear that some were plotting to take the life of Jesus and of Lazarus? I think she may very well have seen the thunderclouds rolling in, the storm on the horizon, and was quite purposeful in what she did.

I'd like to consider Mary's life in the context of John 15, a cornerstone passage in which Jesus tells us how to have a fruitful life, how to understand spiritual mysteries, and how to move into a deeper level of intimacy with Him.

Review your memory verse. A possible prayer for your time with God would be "Open Our Eyes, Lord" (see Appendix A).

14. What stood out to you from today's introduction?

_____

_____

15. Read John 15:1–8.

A. Who is the true vine, who is the gardener, and who are the branches?

_____

B. What must a person do in order to bear fruit? (v. 5) What will make her even more fruitful? (v. 2b)

_____

_____

B. How did you see Mary abiding? How did you see her being pruned? What fruit did you see in her life?

_____

_____

_____

C. What promise is made in verse 7? What is the condition?

_____

_____

16. Read John 15:9–17.

A. Jesus makes an amazing statement in verse 9. How does this show the depth of His love for you? Are you becoming more confident of His love? Explain.

_____

_____

B. What blessings are promised in verses 10 and 11? What is the condition of the blessings?

_____

_____

C. Similarly, John tells us in his letter that the main way to increase our confidence in God's love and in our relationship with Him is through our obedience to His Word (1 John 2:5). Have you experienced this? If so, give an example and comment.

_____

_____

D. How do you think Mary of Bethany's confidence in the love of Jesus for her and in her relationship with Him was strengthened by the breaking of her alabaster bottle?

_____

_____

E. What makes someone "a friend of God"? (v. 14)

_____

_____

F. What privilege does a friend have that a servant does not have? (v. 15)

_____

_____

G. To whom do you reveal your secrets? To whom do you not?

_____

_____

Jesus called Lazarus His "friend" (John 11:11). Might He not have found an openness and an obedience in this home that was remarkable? The psalmist tells us that "the secret of the LORD is with those who fear Him" (Psalm 25:14 NKJV). The Lord also says, "I live in a high and holy place, but also with him who is contrite and lowly in spirit" (Isaiah 57:15b).

H. Do you think Mary of Bethany understood that she was anointing Jesus for His burial? Why or why not?

_____

_____

I. Do you want to be a friend of God? Do you want Him to confide in you? How is this passage speaking to you?

_____

_____

DAY 5

You Are So Beautiful

Individuals who are abandoned to Jesus stand out. A woman who always intrigued me (Kathy) is Mother Teresa. When I heard she was going to be at a 7:30 A.M. mass in New Jersey, I got up at 4:30 A.M. to go and see her. I knew she was getting old and I wanted a chance to encounter her in this life. Church was packed. On either side of the altar, the press was everywhere—ABC, CBS, CNN. In walked Mother Teresa, tiny, worn, and wrinkled. Oh, the glory that emanated from her soul. I was sitting three-fourths of the way back watching and thinking: *This woman who gave her life for the gospel is being praised not only by the church but by the press.* It's just as the Scripture says, "Whoever humbles himself will be exalted." Her abandoned life to Christ has given them something to talk about. Mother Teresa spread His fragrance to the world. Was it Giorgio? Givenchy? Estée Lauder? No—it was Jesus. Jesus was so evident in her, His life so undeniable in her.

God allowed me a special moment I'll never forget. The church service ended and people were leaving in droves. Because of all the paparazzi, frail Mother Teresa was whisked out a back entrance, away from the crowd. I was walking slowly back to my car when all of a sudden I saw a church van pulling away. In the backseat was Mother Teresa. I ran up to the van and spread out my hand on the window. She eagerly reached up and placed her hand on mine. That famous wide smile took hold of her face. I smiled back.

We're living in a time when laser surgery, face-lifts, breast implants, liposuctions, and tummy tucks are readily available. But the most beautiful women I've met have been those women who have surrendered so totally to Jesus that He radiates through their person. He is their beauty. The latest in hair styles, cosmetics, or skin care can never compete or compare with the loveliness of a woman who has allowed Jesus to occupy every place in her heart. How I yearn to be a woman like that. I want to give people something to talk about—and that something, that Someone, is Jesus. That's what Mary of Bethany did, and we can too, if we trust Him and abandon ourselves to Him.

When Mary of Bethany breaks her alabaster bottle at Jesus' feet, He heaps praise upon her, saying, "She has done a beautiful thing to me" (Mark 14:6b). When the Shulammite maiden, in the Song of Songs, abandons herself to her bridegroom by leaving her hiding places and following him, he says: "All beautiful you are, my darling; there is no flaw in you" (Song of Songs 4:7).

We have purposely saved Song of Songs 4:6–18 for the last lesson of this week. Not all will get this far, but perhaps those who do are more likely to be endeavoring to have a deeper walk and are ready for the mysteries in this passage. If that is you, ask the Lord to open your eyes and help you to see.

Just as a bridegroom delights in his bride, so Jesus delights in the Bride who has abandoned herself to Him. It may seem hard to imagine that the Lord would find anything in us in which to delight, but He does. Charles Spurgeon helps us to understand:

> It is very wonderful that we should have within us anything in which God can take delight; yet when we think of all the other wonders of his grace, we need not marvel at all. The God who gave us faith may well be pleased with faith. The God who created love in such unlovely hearts as ours may well be delighted at his own creation.[8]

Review your memory verse.

17. What do you think makes a woman truly beautiful?

_____

_____

18. Read Song of Songs 4:6–8.

   A. In the past, the Shulammite has been hesitant to go higher with her bride-groom. What growth do you see in her? (v. 6)

   _____

   B. What is myrrh associated with in John 19:38–40? What do you think the mountain of myrrh represents?

   _____

This passage contains obvious associations between myrrh and death, and many believe myrrh therefore represents dying to self. Others note that myrrh was used to purify the body, so associate it with the purification that comes as a result of dying to ourselves.

   C. What is the mountain of myrrh in your life right now? Where is Jesus asking you to die, to break an "alabaster bottle"?

   _____

   D. How does the bridegroom respond to the Shulammite's abandonment? (v. 7)

   _____

   E. As in *Hinds' Feet in High Places*, verse 8 pictures the beloved moving from one mountaintop to another with her lover. She is in the high places; she is in the land of invincible love. Yet even in the land of invincible love, there are dangers. How can you see them at the close of verse 8?

   _____

   _____

19. Read Song of Songs 4:9–16.

   A. What two names does Solomon use for the Shulammite in verses 9 and 10? What tenderness, what intimacy does each of these imply?

   _____

   _____

   B. Initially, the Shulammite told Solomon that his kisses were sweeter than wine. (1:2) What does he now tell *her*? (v. 4:10)

   _____

   C. Initially, the Shulammite told Solomon that his fragrance was pleasing, his name was like perfume poured out. (1:3) What does he now tell *her*? (v. 4:11)

> In calling His loved one to a position of spiritual elevation, the Lord did not say that from this time forth everything would be bright and beautiful. He shows her that though the mountaintop life was to be her sphere of movement, yet nevertheless it was a realm where lions and leopards, representative of malignant powers, were close at hand. . . . a spiritually elevated man knows how real and near is the presence of the enemy.[9]
>
> —Watchman Nee

_____

_____

D. Images of intimacy and secrecy are in verse 12, as they are in Proverbs 5:15–18. What do you learn from these pictures about how faithfulness and purity lead to intimacy?

_____

_____

E. The bride's garden is abundant with fruit, flowing with spices. (v. 13) As you are learning to abandon yourself to the Lord, what fruit have you seen that He might delight in?

_____

_____

F. What kind of wind is the wind from the north? What kind of wind is the wind from the south? What do you think these represent? (v. 16)

_____

_____

G. Give an example of how the chilling and bitter experiences of life have brought forth fruit in your life.

_____

_____

H. Give an example of how the sweet and gentle gifts of God have brought forth fruit in your life.

_____

_____

Finale

REVIEW

20. Each woman should share one thing that God impressed on her heart from this study, one way she was "kissed by the King."

PRAYER

Read your answer to question 18C if you are willing. Allow the other women to support you with sentence prayers. Then support them as they read their answers.

Our Love Is Here to Stay

Prelude

This is a profound mystery . . .
—Ephesians 5:32a

What is a profound mystery? Marriage, in an amazing way, is meant to be a foreshadowing of our relationship with Jesus. Earthly bridegrooms are to love their wives sacrificially, in the same way that Jesus loved His Bride.

> *Husbands, love your wives, just as Christ loved the church and gave himself up for her to make her holy, cleansing her by the washing with water through the word, and to present her to himself as a radiant church, without stain or wrinkle or any other blemish, but holy and blameless.* (Ephesians 5:25–27)

Husbands who have this kind of sacrificial love are rare, but they do exist. One of the reasons we believe that the award-winning Italian film *Life Is Beautiful* struck such a chord in the hearts of viewers is because it vividly shows us this kind of love. Though we don't agree with everything in the film, still, the central message is profound. It beautifully portrays the love of the bridegroom for his bride and her response to his amazing love. We see it as a meaningful parable that can shed light on the profound mystery Paul writes about.

As Christ woos us, the husband wooed his wife-to-be in *Life Is Beautiful*. He called her "Principessa" (Princess) and wooed her by surprising her, by making her laugh, and by treating her like royalty. He was so tender, so creative, and so persistent in winning her heart. He rescued her from marrying a brutish man, from her own selfishness, and finally, from the greatest horror of the twentieth century, the holocaust against the Jews and those who tried to protect them. It meant laying down his life for his wife and son, but his love caused him to do it.

For a man like this, you would do anything.

WATCH VIDEO #9: OUR LOVE IS HERE TO STAY
Dee will be teaching from Ruth.

_____

_____

_____

_____

GROUP RESPONSE TO THE VIDEO

A. What are some ways that God "played the music," even in the bleakest of circumstances, for Naomi?

B. What stood out to you from the video?

C. How might you apply this teaching to your life?

DAY 1

When a Man Loves a Woman

When I (Kathy) became a Christian, my friends said, "Are you kidding me? Do you know what the Bible says about men and women and about submission? What are you doing, Troccoli? You're going backward."

I tried to make them understand. I said, "Look, you can't just pick out one piece of Scripture and not acknowledge the words around it. That's like trying to understand the beauty of a rose garden by looking at a single thorn. It clearly tells husbands to love their wives as Christ loved the church. That is such a high calling, and it is so sacrificial. Christ gave His life for the church. I would love to experience that kind of lavishness from a man. Can't you see?" I knew they weren't willing to see. That was really my very first glimpse that if you don't know the whole of Scripture, you can twist it and turn it and use it in any way you want. But that doesn't mean it will represent the heart of God. It blows my mind to see women picketing outside Promise Keepers' rallies. They are protesting the gift God is yearning to bestow on them—the gift of a man loving Jesus with all his heart, humbling himself before God, sacrificing his own pride, making a commitment to die to himself. Why would anybody have a problem with that? That's what I love about *Life Is Beautiful*. It is the epitome of a husband imitating Jesus Christ, laying down his life for his bride.

I (Dee) remember a pivotal time early in my marriage. Steve and I were deep in the wilderness as Steve was going through his ninety-hour-a-week internship in Seattle. I was a believer, but an immature one, and I thought: *What good does it do me to be married if my husband is never around?* I also felt that if Steve really truly loved me he would find a way to beat the system that prepared individuals to be doctors. I expressed all these feelings to Steve.

Fortunately, Steve was godly enough to listen to me. Though my husband was young in his faith, the way he responded to me showed me Jesus. Steve came to me the next day and said he couldn't see a way to change his situation as a medical intern. Before I could begin ranting and raving again, he said, "I love you and I care more about you and our marriage than my dream of being a surgeon. I am willing to give that up."

I was stunned as I thought about the sacrifice he was sincerely offering. Steve had already completed seven years of training, but I knew he was speaking the truth because he, unlike me, was truly Christlike in the way of honesty. His willingness to sacrifice for me inspired me to sacrifice for him. I wept and told him that I loved him too, and that I would support him, and that we would make it through that year, and that he wouldn't hear any talk of ending our marriage ever again. For me, it was the beginning of learning to submit, to support my husband, even when it meant dying to my own wants. I was learning to obey what Peter wrote:

> Be good wives to your husbands, responsive to their needs. (1 Peter 3:1 MSG)

Submission is a difficult concept. Kathy found an anonymous quote we love:

> Where He leads me, I will follow
> What He feeds me, I will swallow.

Submission is one of the harder truths to swallow. In part (though only in part), I think that is because it is misunderstood. I was motivated to write the Bible study guide *A Woman's Journey through 1 Peter* to help women explore in depth this concept of submission. Though we cannot look at 1 Peter in that kind of depth in this study, we can at least look at this "thorn" in the context of the whole rose garden.

Learn your final memory verse (next week is review):

> Many waters cannot quench love;
>   rivers cannot wash it away. (Song of Songs 8:7a)

1. How can a good marriage be a dim reflection of the relationship Christ has with His Bride?

   _____

   _____

2. What stood out to you from the examples from *Life Is Beautiful* and Dee's marriage?

   _____

   _____

3. The primary example of submission is Christ Himself. In 1 Peter 2:21–24, find all the ways Christ submitted because of His love for us.

_____

_____

4. How was He able to remain silent in the face of such injustice? (1 Peter 2:23b)

_____

_____

5. In each of these passages, who is told to follow in the steps of Christ and to submit?

   A. 1 Peter 2:13–15_____

   B. 1 Peter 2:18_____

   C. 1 Peter 3:1–2_____

   D. 1 Peter 3:7_____

   Note the phrase repeated from 1 Peter 3:1, "In the same way."

   E. 1 Peter 3:8–9_____

Two common errors that a woman can make concerning submission in marriage are:

1. Pretending to submit but covertly trying to get her own way through manipulation or deceit.
2. Being completely passive and relinquishing her mind, making her husband shoulder all the decisions and responsibility for both of them.

We are called to be "co-heirs" (1 Peter 3:7) and, together, to seek God's will. We are called to be honest, and to speak the truth in love. If we sense our husband is out of God's will, we have a responsibility to say so. In the book *Boundaries*, the authors give wisdom to the woman who is married to a controlling husband. If he is taking advantage of her submissive position and asking her to do things that are wrong, or to support him in things that are wrong, she has a responsibility to God to lovingly but firmly set a boundary.[1] (For example, "I love you, but I will not lie to your boss about your drinking.") We are to submit in everything except sin. I (Dee) believe that often submission has been given a bad name because it has been misunderstood or misapplied.

In a healthy marriage, submission is beautiful, and it goes both ways, for we are told:

Submit to one another out of reverence for Christ. (Ephesians 5:21)

But it is also true that God particularly directs wives to submit. This does not mean that a wife is inferior, for we are told that Christ submitted to God. But it is God's plan that a husband be a servant leader and that his wife be supportive of that leadership.

> *Now as the church submits to Christ, so also wives should submit to their husbands in everything.* (Ephesians 5:24)

This is a profound mystery, but earthly brides are a foreshadowing of the ultimate Bride, the Bride of Christ. As we learn to submit to others on earth, we are also being fashioned to become the Bride of Christ. And never, ever was there a Bridegroom like Jesus.

Day 2

I'd Do Anything

In *Life Is Beautiful,* to the amazement of the Nazi guards, the "Principessa" insisted on stopping and boarding a train headed to the death camps. Why? Her husband and son were on it. She was willing to do anything, even give up her life, for this man and for their child.

As believers, we will make sacrifices the world will not understand, because of our love for Christ. And, as we die to ourselves and submit to Him, we will also experience a joy and a peace the world can never know. We will also discover a transformation in our hearts, for, as we learn to submit to the Lord, we will become radiant, holy, and blameless.

A transformation took place in Ruth as she stepped out in faith and followed Naomi and Naomi's God. God had declared, concerning the Moabites:

> *No Ammonite or Moabite or any of his descendants may enter the assembly of the LORD, even down to the tenth generation.* (Deuteronomy 23:3)

Yet Ruth not only enters in, she becomes an ancestor of Jesus Christ, our Lord. Her name is listed in the Christ's geneology in the opening of Matthew. Do you know why?

It is because she was no longer a Moabite. She was washed; she was whiter than snow. And as she followed the one true God, dying to herself and submitting to Him, He fashioned her into an absolutely breathtaking bride, holy and blameless in His sight. She stood out among believers, and everyone was talking about her.

Read Ruth 1 and 2 as a review. Also, review your memory verse from Week 4.

Entreat me not to leave thee, or to return from following after thee: for whither thou goest, I will go; and where thou lodgest, I will lodge: thy people shall be my people, and thy God my God:

Where thou diest, will I die, and there will I be buried: the LORD do so to me and more also, if ought but death part thee and me. (Ruth 1:16–17 KJV)

6. According to Ruth 1:16–17 and 2:11, what were some of the sacrifices Ruth made in order to follow Naomi and Naomi's God?

    _____

    _____

7. Ruth's inner beauty was evident to the townspeople. What comment was made about her, and by whom, in the following passages?

    A. Ruth 2:6–7_____

    _____

    B. Ruth 2:11_____

    _____

    C. Ruth 3:11_____

    _____

    D. Ruth 4:15_____

    _____

Obedience is a result of spiritual growth, but spiritual growth is also a result of obedience. The more you submit, the more you step out on faith, the more you are empowered to go higher.

8. In the following passages, what result follows obedience?

    A. 1 John 2:5 _____

    _____

    B. 1 John 2:10a _____

    _____

    C. 1 John 2:28_____

    _____

    D. 1 John 3:16–20_____

    _____

9. Are you experiencing any of the above results in your life as you abandon your-self to Him? Explain.

_____

_____

_____

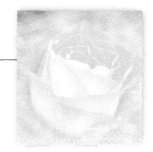

DAY 3

I Write the Songs

In the concentration camp in *Life Is Beautiful,* the woman is separated from her husband and little boy. She doesn't know if they have survived. Yet they *are* alive. Her husband has managed to survive and also to keep their five-year-old son safe. He has told their little boy that the concentration camp is a great game in which he can accumulate points by hiding, by being very quiet, and by not crying for his mommy.

The "Principessa" hears that the children have been taken into what they thought were showers and murdered through gas coming through the shower heads. She sees a huge pile of children's clothing. She sinks to her knees and begins looking through it, hoping against hope that she won't find a familiar little shirt and shorts.

Suddenly, she hears her husband's voice over the broadcast system of the concentration camp:

> "Principessa! I dreamt about you all last night. You were wearing that pink suit I love. . . ."

And then she hears her little boy's voice:

> "Mama! Mama! Daddy is hiding me in the wheelbarrow—and he doesn't know how to drive the wheelbarrow—and we laugh like crazy."

Great relief floods through her as she realizes that they are still alive.

Another time the husband is busing tables for the Nazi guards. He spies a Victrola and finds the record that they listened to when they were falling in love. He turns the amplifying horn toward the window, facing her barracks, and the romantic melody wafts out over the grim surroundings. She wakes, and hears the music. Slowly she climbs down from her bunk, tears welling in her eyes as she realizes that it has to be him who is playing this song. *He is still alive! He still loves me! And he has found a way to play the music for me.*

Essentially, this is the picture in the Book of Ruth. Naomi, in this case, is the "Principessa." She has suffered so much, and yet, the Lord finds a way to play the music for her. At first she cannot hear it, even when Ruth makes her tremendous commitment of "Whither thou goest. . . ." Naomi is so broken that she is silent, trudging on to Bethlehem, her heart full of bitterness and anger.

But, as the story continues, and the Lord's mercies continue, the music grows louder and louder until finally Naomi hears. She lifts her eyes to heaven and says:

> He [my God] *has not stopped showing His kindness to the living and the dead.* (Ruth 2:20)

Though most of us will not have to endure the horrors that Naomi endured, life is full of trouble. Even when we reach the height of invincible love, we are still in this world and we will still have tears, pain, and death. But in the midst of that, a woman can have peace, because she knows she is His beloved princess. And if she gets quiet enough, Jesus will come. He will play the music.

We also can have confidence that one day He will come thundering through the sky to take us to a place where there is no more crying, no more sorrow, and no more death.

Review the following two verses:

> *The* LORD *your God is with you,*
> *he is mighty to save.*
> *He will take great delight in you,*
> *he will quiet you with his love,*
> *he will rejoice over you with singing.* (Zephaniah 3:17)

> *Many waters cannot quench love;*
> *rivers cannot wash it away.* (Song of Songs 8:7a)

10. In the midst of sorrow on earth, Jesus calls, "Principessa!" He longs to protect each of us. He gave His life for us. He couldn't bear to spend eternity without us. It is because of His mercies that we are not consumed. Morning by morning His mercies are new. Morning by morning His music brings hope. Share a time when, in the bleakest of circumstances, God played the music for you, when He quieted you with His love. How did He do it?

_____

_____

Naomi has often been called a female version of Job. She suffered so much. The opening six verses of the Book of Ruth are one piercing arrow after another into Naomi's heart. They begin with a famine in the land, and the situation gets bleaker with each verse. It is important to remember that God had promised that if His people were faithful, He would not send a famine (Deuteronomy 11:13–15). He had also told His people not to intermarry with unbelievers. The Moabites worshipped gods who demanded sexual immorality and child sacrifice.

11. Try, in each of the following circumstances, to imagine why what happened was painful to Naomi, and how she must have felt.

   A. *there was a famine in the land.* (Ruth 1:1a)

   _____

   _____

   B. *And they went to Moab and lived there.* (Ruth 1:2c)

   _____

   _____

   C. *Now Elimelech, Naomi's husband, died, and she was left with her two sons.* (Ruth 1:3)

   _____

   _____

   D. *They married Moabite women.* (Ruth 1:4)

   _____

   _____

   E. *After they had lived there about ten years, both Mahlon and Kilion also died, and Naomi was left without her two sons and her husband.* (Ruth 1:4b–5)

   _____

   _____

One of the beautiful images in the Book of Ruth is the transformation from barrenness to fruitfulness. The book begins with "a famine in the land." However, by the close of the first chapter, "the barley harvest was beginning." The harvest is rich and plentiful as God "plays the music," louder and louder, throughout the book.

In the same way, we see a transformation in Naomi from barrenness to fruitfulness as God's mercies begin and increase throughout the book. In the first chapter, despite Ruth's famous commitment, Naomi is unable to hear the music.

12. In the following passages, what does Naomi say that shows barrenness and bitterness? Try to put yourself in her place and describe her emotions.

   A. Ruth 1:1 _____

   _____

B. Ruth 1:12–13 _____

_____

C. Ruth 1:15 _____

_____

D. Ruth 1:20–21 _____

_____

13. In the following passages, how do you see God "playing the music" for Naomi in greater and greater intensity?

A. Ruth 1:6 _____

B. Ruth 1:16–17 _____

_____

C. Ruth 1:22 _____

D. Ruth 2:1–3 _____

_____

E. Ruth 2:4 _____

F. Ruth 2:17–20 _____

_____

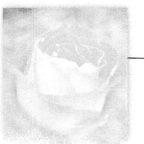

DAY 4

Ain't No Mountain High Enough

Sometimes the problems in our lives seem insurmountable. Naomi had given up, feeling her life was over. Yet God found a way to get to her, and He can find a way to get to you as well. You are His Princess, His Beloved, the object of His affection.

As Benigni, the husband in *Life Is Beautiful*, played the music for his wife, I (Dee) was reminded of the times in my life when I was desperate: when my Dad was having triple bypass surgery and I feared he didn't know the Lord; when our son was rebelling against the Lord; when I felt betrayed by one I thought would never betray me. I (Kathy) remember the time in my life when I was in such despair that I lay on a couch for three days and just didn't want to get up; when my mom was dying; when I felt at the end of my rope in my career.

Somehow or other, the Lord always finds a way to comfort us, to play the music for us.

Sometimes it is through His presence, so real, so tangible. Recently, I (Kathy) was home in Long Island, dealing with a fresh disappointment in my life. Curling up, I put my head on my pillow and wept. All of a sudden I felt like I was resting my head on Jesus' lap. I could almost feel His tender hands gently stroking my hair. I knew He was wiping my tears. He'd heard my prayers.

Review the following verse:

> Even though I walk
>   through the valley of the shadow of death,
> I will fear no evil,
>   for you are with me;
> your rod and your staff,
>   they comfort me. (Psalm 23:4)

14. Is there a problem in your life that sometimes seems insurmountable? What is it?

_____

_____

15. Think about problems in your past that seemed insurmountable, yet Jesus overcame them. List one.

_____

_____

Like Solomon in the Song of Songs, now it is Boaz who comes leaping across the mountains to rescue his princess. Of course, as in every great love story, there is an obstacle. But Boaz, our Christ figure, is up to the challenge. The story is full of intrigue. Read Ruth 3 and 4 as an overview.

16. By this point in the story, Naomi has "heard the music," and she has a renewed confidence. What evidence can you find in the following passages that she has come out of her depression?

A. Ruth 2:22_____

_____

B. Ruth 3:1–4_____

_____

*From the Wenzel Bible,
a fourteenth-century painting of Ruth
sleeping at the feet of Boaz.*[xiii]

ൟ

*Notice how this ancient painting portrays night,
the abundance of the harvest, the surprise
of Boaz, and the purity of Ruth.*

Naomi's plan sounds quite strange to us. Why would she ask Ruth to creep out under the black Bethlehem sky and go to where Boaz is sleeping, guarding the grain, and uncover his feet? Remember that Boaz was their "kinsman-redeemer." For whatever reason, he has not yet asked Ruth to marry him. Perhaps he is unsure of her feelings for him. Perhaps he is aware that there is a nearer kinsman and feels it is therefore not his place to ask Ruth to marry him. In any case, this plan is meant to encourage Boaz. Ruth is making her feelings known, and Naomi is confident Boaz will act appropriately.

17. When Ruth uncovers the feet of Boaz, he wakes. What question does he ask, and how does she respond? What do you think he is really asking? (Ruth 3:9–10)

_____

_____

J. Vernon McGee explains that after Boaz had shown an interest in Ruth, according to the Mosaic system, it was incumbent upon Ruth to make a definite move. If she didn't, it would have constituted rejection of Boaz as a suitor. When Ruth pulled the end of the long mantle covering Boaz over herself, she was asking him to be her shelter and protection, to be her husband.[2] Some erroneously believe she was asking him to make love to her, but that is out of character with the integrity of both Ruth and Boaz. Cyril Barber gives further corroboration of their purity:

> The Hebrew word *lun*, "to pass the night," has latent within it the passage of time and does not concern itself with the manner in which the time was spent. If Boaz and Ruth had engaged in sexual relations on the threshing floor then *sakab*, "to lie (together), to sleep (together)" would have been used. *Lun* is a word devoid of sexual connotations.[3]

18. There is an obstacle to the marriage. What is it, according to Ruth 3:12–13?

_____

_____

19. In Ruth 3:16–18, how do you see confidence in the words of both Ruth and Naomi?

_____

_____

The land of invincible love is not a land that is free of problems, but it is a land full of confidence.

20. Boaz masterfully overcomes the obstacle of the other man, the nearer kinsman-redeemer. Apparently he knows something about the character of this man and suspects he will be interested in acquiring the land, but not in acquiring a Moabite bride.

   A. How does Boaz make sure there are witnesses to this dialogue? (Ruth 4:1–2)

   _____

   _____

   B. What part of the transaction does Boaz tell the man about? What part does he skillfully omit? (Ruth 4:3–4)

   _____

   C. How does the nearer kinsman respond at first? (Ruth 4:4b) How does he respond when he realizes Ruth the Moabitess is part of the bargain? (vv. 5–6)

   _____

   _____

There is humor in the above. Can't you imagine Boaz saying the word *Moabitess* quite clearly and loudly? He has managed to reveal this man's true motives. The nearer kinsman is interested in the land, but not in the responsibility of caring for a Moabitess widow. He is concerned about his reputation and his inheritance, but not about his responsibility.

D. Ruth 4:7–8 needs to be understood in the context of Deuteronomy 25:5–10. Read this and explain the disgrace of the nearer kinsman's refusal.

_____

_____

E. Describe the emotion in the proclamation of Boaz in Ruth 4:9–10? How has he been an exemplary Prince Charming?

_____

_____

21. Have you grown in your confidence that Jesus will come through for you? If so, how?

_____

_____

DAY 5

May I Be His Love for You

Love is the mark of a Christian because God is love. We can't, in the flesh, love those who are hard to love—but God can. Our lack of love, or our lack of gentleness, or our lack of compassion can cling to us like stubborn leaves that cling to branches throughout the fall and winter. It isn't until spring, when the sap rises, that those leaves are finally pushed off. In the same way, we may want, in our flesh, to love somebody who is hard to love, but we just can't. So we earnestly pray that God will fill us with love for that person. Then one day, we realize that His love has had His way in us. The sap has risen and pushed those ugly leaves off. I (Dee) experienced that with our daughter Beth. When we adopted her, as a twelve-year-old, I showed her kindness, but genuine love wasn't really in me. I asked God for it, but I was still so easily irritated with her. And then one day, when someone hurt her feelings because of her missing arm, I became like a mother bear. And I realized, *I really love this child. I'm not just* showing *her love. I love her!* And though I can still become irritated with her, there is a genuine change in my attitude toward her. And I have found that as I play games with her, or hide a little surprise under her pillow, or tell her what I like in her, my love for her actually increases. John explains it like this:

God is love. Whoever lives in love lives in God, and God in him. (1 John 4:16b)

And I know, also, that my only hope of embracing my eighty-seven-year-old father with the love of Jesus is to show him that love. When he raises his voice at me (because old age is like walking through a minefield and he is grieving the loss of health, of friends, of independence), when he is outraged that I insist on driving the car (because he'll kill us all if he drives), when he barks at my grown children to "Get off the phone!" (because they don't know the value of a dollar), I absolutely have to respond in love. I can be firm, but I must be kind. I can disagree, but I must be respectful. I must be the love of Jesus to him. It amazes me that in the midst of these stressful situations, God gives me His peace and perspective. He is helping me to realize how precious Dad is to me—and to remember that one day I, too, may need a whole lot of grace. I am falling back. He is catching me.

I (Kathy) used to have such a problem with anger. Even my mother, though she mellowed, could get extremely angry and upset about tiny little things. I had such tension with my mother in my teens, and to this day, I could weep about it. One time I even pushed her up against the wall, I was so out of control. She didn't know how to handle me, and I didn't know how to handle her. Those were not easy times in our lives. I was so unruly, my mother used to have my uncles come and talk to me, since my dad had died. Anger was so ingrained in me that it was my natural response to problems.

When I first met the Lord, it was the start of my praying to be more graceful, gentle, and kind. I yearned to be like some of the women I'd read about in Scripture and some of the women I was meeting who truly clothed themselves in Christ. When I look at myself objectively, I can see how God has done a great work in me. Sometimes I am even shocked at the days and the weeks and the months that go by. Though I can get frustrated, there's not this rage that I used to feel. I'm so much more consistent. Sometimes when I go home to New York I get together with my large extended family. I find myself getting startled when they shout at each other, "Pass the buttah!" That way of communicating, though endearing in those settings, is not the way I live anymore. Those waves of anger that used to come in and destroy everything around me are now so much more subdued. His presence comes over me and checks me. I know I'm a miracle.

One of the clearest signs that we have reached the land of invincible love is when His love is consistently flowing out of us to others, no matter how lovely or unlovely they are. Kathy expresses this beautifully in her song "May I Be His Love." I (Dee) think of Ruth loving Naomi every time she sings it. It's a beautiful prayer. As you read the lyrics, think about the people God has put in your life, and make this your prayer:

May I be His love for you
May I lift your eyes toward heaven
May I come to you and lead you to His light
May I cry His tears for you
May I be the place that you can run to
Where you'll hear His voice
And see Him in my eyes
All your life
May I be His love

Review this week's memory verse:

Many waters cannot quench love;
rivers cannot wash it away. (Song of Songs 8:7a)

22. One of the clear goals of Ruth's life was to fill the empty arms of Naomi. Describe how she did it in the following passages:

A. Ruth 1:16–17_____

B. Ruth 2:17–18_____

C. Ruth 3:16–17_____

D. Ruth 4:13–17_____

23. In herself Ruth was unable to fill the empty arms of Naomi. It was because of the Lord's faithfulness to Ruth that she was equipped to be His love to Naomi. How do you see faithfulness from the Lord to Ruth in the following passages?

A. Ruth 2:3_____

B. Ruth 2:14–16_____

C. Ruth 3:11a_____

D. Ruth 3:14_____

E. Ruth 4:13_____

The Book of Hosea, like the Song of Songs and the Book of Ruth, shows us that though we will go through the wilderness, the Lord will come to us, if we press on, if we do not lose hope. The fruit of that persistence is that His love will overwhelm us; as surely as the sun rises, He will appear.

24. Meditate on Hosea 6:1–3.

A. What does Hosea encourage God's people to do, and why? (v. 1)

_____

_____

B. Will restoration occur immediately? What symbolism do you see in verse 2?

_____

_____

C. What does Hosea encourage God's people to do in the opening of verse 3?

_____

D. What word pictures are given in verse 3 to give us confidence in the Lord?

_____

_____

25. As God has filled you with His love, watered you with His spring rain, how have you seen changes in your relationship with others?

_____

_____

Finale

REVIEW

26. Each woman should share, if she chooses, one way she was "kissed by the King" in this study.

PRAYER

Is there an area where you need the Lord to come through for you, to "play the music" for you? Cluster in fours and lift up your need in prayer. Let the other women support you with sentence prayers.

All Is Well

❧

Orchestra
allegro scherzando
(Begin briskly, keeping the tempo lively)

adagio expressivo
(Slowly move into a somber mood)

tranquillo risoluto
(Close peacefully but with passionate confidence)

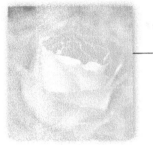

WEEK 10

All Is Well

Prelude

When I (Kathy) first moved to Nashville in my twenties, my family had such high hopes and dreams for me. I was managed by the same men who managed Amy Grant, and that started the whole process of God humbling me. When I was in Long Island I was the big fish in the small pond, and now I was watching Nashville's princess walk through my dreams. I started working in a little Christian bookstore, and my family couldn't understand why things weren't happening. I did get out my first recording, *Stubborn Love*, in 1982. I'm not saying I didn't have a certain amount of success at that time, because I did. But it didn't quite happen the way I thought it was going to. All these years later, I realize that God was protecting me from having too much too soon. I realize now that God was developing a holy brokenness and humility in me that could not have happened had I not lived through that season in my life. I've often hung on to Mother Teresa's words: "Faithfulness, not success." God is sovereign. And whether or not I ever sing another note, I am God's Beloved. He desires a relationship with me. That is the most important thing.

At this time in my life, God is allowing me to step into arenas where I am speaking and singing to thousands of women. My spirit often says, "Ahhhh." The years of feeling like things should be happening in a certain way (ways I had imagined), the years of feeling forgotten by God, feeling like a stepchild, have prepared me for such a time as this. He's patiently loved me and taught me and revealed Himself to me. And that is how I'm able to speak to women boldly and confidently about Jesus. Whether I'm addressing eating disorders, self-esteem, death, bitterness toward an ex-husband, an abortion, or the hundred other things women face every day of their lives, the solution is the same. The answer is the same. We must know God. We must be honest with Him. We must be willing to pick up the cross He offers us, knowing there will always be a resurrection. Always.

Do Dee and I still get frustrated? Do we still question God? Do I still have days when lifting my head from the pillow feels like an impossible chore? Absolutely. We're trapped in these bodies, and we will deal with these things until we see Him face to face. Until then, we must cling desperately to the One who is crazy about us, to the One who has promised us wholeness, to the One who has promised never to let us go.

This week we are going to do a review of the vital truths we've studied in His Word. Because we are human, we have to keep reviewing, we have to keep remembering why we fell in love with Jesus, we have to keep going over what He taught us in the wilderness, and we absolutely must keep abandoning ourselves to the One who will always catch us. When we do that, no matter what trials we must face, we will find that all is well.

No Video This Week
Use all your time in review.

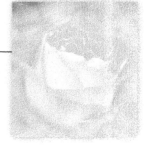

DAY 1

Someday My Prince Will Come

From the time you were a little girl, God has been wooing you. He knit you together in your mother's womb. He made you. He knows you. And He knows how to talk to you. His goal is to win you, and one day, to wed you. This study has repeatedly looked at the theme of romance in Scripture, at the picture of Jesus as your Bridegroom and you as the Bride, the object of His affection. Our goal for this entire study is that you would begin to look at Jesus in a new way and yearn for an intimacy that you had not known before. As you review this theme today, consider how you have moved toward that goal.

Review this memory verse:

> *As a bridegroom rejoices over his bride,*
> *so will your God rejoice over you.* (Isaiah 62:5b)

1. Meditate on Isaiah 62:5b.

    A. Describe how you imagine a bridegroom feels the moment the bride enters the church sanctuary and walks down the aisle toward him. Describe also how he feels, if they have lived purely, about finally being able to take her home.

    _____

    _____

    _____

    B. Are you growing in your confidence that Jesus loves you like this? In the last ten weeks, how has He awakened you to the reality of His love?

_____

_____

C. In *Snow White* and *Sleeping Beauty*, the prince awakens his love with a kiss. Can you think of a "kiss" from the King that awakened you in the last ten weeks? Consider particularly a revelation of truth from His Word that has awakened you, His sleeping princess.

_____

_____

2. Review the parts of the Jewish wedding ceremony and their symbolism (see Day 1 of Week 4).

A. What was the *erusin* ("forbidden") or betrothal time? How binding was it? How is this significant to us spiritually? (Hosea 2:19–20)

_____

_____

B. What did the bridegroom do during the period of separation? What did the bride do? How is this significant to us spiritually? (John 14:1–4)

_____

_____

C. What was the *nissuin* ("carrying" or "taking")? What feelings does this evoke in you? How is this significant to us spiritually? (See Revelation 19:6–8 and Psalm 45.)

_____

_____

Review this memory verse:

> The LORD your God is with you,
>   he is mighty to save.
>   He will take great delight in you,
> he will quiet you with his love,
>   he will rejoice over you with singing. (Zephaniah 3:17)

3. What thoughts do you have as you meditate on the above? Are the truths of the above verse becoming more of a reality to you? Explain.

_____

_____

4. How did you see the above passage exemplified by the Lord's care for two of His brides: Elizabeth and Mary? What do you remember about the Lord's deliverance of each of them, His delight in them, and His creativity in "playing the music" for them (see Week 2)?

_____

_____

DAY 2

Looking for Love in All the Wrong Places

Though we have an absolutely faithful Bridegroom, we are unfaithful brides. A persistent theme throughout Scripture is that we break the heart of our Bridegroom by running after other lovers. As said earlier, Philip Yancey says, "The words of the prophets sound like the words of a lover's quarrel drifting through thin apartment walls."[1] We studied the life of Solomon, and then, in Week 6, the life of Jacob. And if we are honest, we saw ourselves. The first step in leading to repentance is learning to recognize when we have made a wrong turn. Today, not only review the lives of these historical men, but also consider how you are like them and how you must guard your heart.

Review this memory verse:

> *Above all else, guard your heart,*
> *for it is the wellspring of life.* (Proverbs 4:23)

5. How did Solomon fail to guard his heart? (1 Kings 11:1–8)

_____

_____

6. Describe some of the false "lovers" that Solomon pursued in Ecclesiastes 2. How did he feel as he was in the midst of each pursuit? Contrast that with his feelings at the end of each pursuit.

_____

_____

7. If you had a movie night, recall the scene in *Camelot* in which Guenevere and Sir

Lancelot sang "I Loved You Once in Silence." How did their feelings during the pursuit and at the close of their pursuit parallel those of Solomon?

_____

_____

8. Where do you tend to look for love in the wrong places? How do you feel during the pursuit? How do you feel afterward?

_____

_____

9. Contrast the above feelings with the feelings you have had when you obeyed the Lord, when you died to yourself. How did you feel during the "death"? How did you feel afterward?

_____

_____

10. How did Jacob look for love in the wrong places? Recall the kinds of pain that came into his life as a result of wrong choice (see Week 6).

_____

_____

11. What do you recall about God's stubborn love for Jacob? How does this encourage you?

_____

_____

12. How did Jacob have to die to himself? How did the Lord bless him when he did?

_____

_____

13. Where is God asking you to die to yourself? What have you learned that will give you the strength to do so?

_____

_____

Love Me Tender

First love is that euphoric time when you can hardly believe that someone so wonderful is interested in you. Just as this happens when you fall in love with an earthly man, the first realization that the God who made the universe is actually *mindful* of you can make you feel like a smitten schoolgirl. Both Kathy and I remember walking on cloud nine, being filled, as Sheldon Vanauken expresses it, with a "kind of hesitant, incredulous wonder. Could this really be happening—this marvel?"[2]

Falling in love is a precious time, never to be forgotten. Though Jesus does not want us to stay in the honeymoon time, He wants us to remember it and keep on remembering it. What was it that caused you to first fall in love with Jesus? What were you like? What did you do? Though we grow in maturity, we should never stop loving Him the way we did at first. Remembering why we fell in love and doing the things we did at first can help us to make it through the wilderness times.

Review this memory verse:

> *Let him kiss me with the kisses of his mouth—*
> *for your love is more delightful than wine.* (Song of Songs 1:2)

14. What were you like when you first fell in love with Jesus? What were some of the things you did? What were some of your feelings?

    _____

    _____

15. Scripture gives us bridegrooms to show us an aspect of the ultimate Bridegroom. One we considered was Boaz, who wooed Ruth, won her, and eventually wed her.

    A. Read Ruth 2:8–9.
       What do you see in Boaz?_____

       _____

       How is Jesus like this?_____

       _____

       Why is this attribute of Jesus precious to you?_____

       _____

B. Read Ruth 2:11–12.
What do you see in Boaz?_____

_____

How is Jesus like this?_____

_____

Why is this attribute of Jesus precious to you?_____

_____

C. Read Ruth 2:14–16.
What do you see in Boaz?_____

_____

How is Jesus like this?_____

_____

Why is this attribute of Jesus precious to you?_____

_____

D. Read Ruth 4:9–10.
What do you see in Boaz?_____

_____

How is Jesus like this?_____

_____

Why is this attribute of Jesus precious to you?_____

_____

16. Recall the feelings Ruth had when she was first aware of the attentions of Boaz.

A. Read Ruth 2:10.
What attitude do you see in Ruth?_____

_____

Did you have any of those same feelings when you first realized Jesus had noticed you? If so, why?

_____

B. Read Ruth 2:21.
What excitement do you see in Ruth as she tells Naomi details about Boaz?

_____

When you were a new believer, did you talk to people about Jesus? What did you tell them?

_____

_____

Review Ruth's famous commitment:

> *Entreat me not to leave thee, or to return from following after thee: for whither thou goest, I will go; and where thou lodgest, I will lodge: thy people shall be my people, and thy God my God:*
> *Where thou diest, will I die, and there will I be buried: the* LORD *do so to me, and more also, if ought but death part thee and me.* (Ruth 1:16–17 KJV)

17. As you look at the above commitment in the context of you, as a believer, saying it to Jesus, what do you see?

_____

_____

18. Recall what Mary of Bethany was like in her first-love time with Jesus. (Luke 11:38–42) Were you like this in your first-love time? Explain.

_____

19. Of what had Martha lost sight? Why did Jesus rebuke her?

_____

_____

20. Review what Jesus said to the believers in Ephesus in Revelation 2:1–7.

    A. How did Jesus praise them? (v. 2)_____

    _____

    B. Yet what did He hold against them? (v. 4)_____

    _____

    C. What three things did He tell them to do? (v. 5)_____

    _____

    D. How could you apply this to your life today?_____

    _____

Killing Me Softly

I (Kathy) often reflect on how God woos me, wins me, and loves me to Himself. Many, many times He works on my heart by breaking my heart. I can't seem to learn any other way. Now, when I think about having to pick up my cross (and I know I'll be picking up a cross), I pray, *Jesus, be merciful to me.*

Jesus *is* incredibly patient and gentle with us. At the same time He is strong and pointed about the things that cause us to commit adultery. We are prone to go after other idols. God is a jealous God. He doesn't want us just to break the idols. He wants us to grind them into powder.

I (Dee) struggled in letting go of each of my two adult sons and, most recently, Sally, my first daughter to leave the nest. Many mothers tend to worship their children, loving them more than God. I've had to ask myself if that is true of me. I thought I *had* let Sally go, so then I wondered: *Why does the pain keep increasing? Why do our phone conversations continue to make me so sad? Why does God seem to keep taking her farther and farther away? Why isn't He making my life turn out the way I expected it to in my relationship with Sally? Is He dealing with me?* Sally and her husband moved to Krakow, Poland, after their marriage. I've had a lot of heartache and have felt much anxiety about her. My husband has said, "You think about her too much, you worry about her too much. You haven't really relinquished her to God, Dee." I remember hearing Corrie ten Boom, who lived out her faith in Nazi concentration camps, say that if we cling to someone or something too tightly, our loving Father will pry our fingers away. In fact, I've told thousands of women that *this* is our weakness as women: We're so relational. We hold our friends, our husbands, and our children too tightly. And so now I wrestle with these questions: *Will I trust God with Sally? Even if, in the future, He allows my beloved child to suffer, will I trust that He is good and that He is God? Will I stop trying to control her life, stop trying to shield her from pain? Will I let go, let her fall, and believe His arms will catch her?* In my heart I say, "Yes." Yet it is a continual relinquishment. I must continually lift her up to God and pray: *Help me to trust You. Help me to let go. And Jesus, please kill me softly. Please be gentle with me.*

Whatever it is in our life that is keeping us from going higher with the Lord needs to be relinquished. Perhaps it is the love of something good, like a child, or a career—a good thing, but something that has become to us what only God can be: security and peace. Perhaps it is a secret sin—the adulterous arms of an addiction, or gluttony, or sexual immorality. Perhaps someone has wronged us and we keep licking our wounds. God wants us to forgive, let go of the wrong, and come higher. These are all hard things to give up, and so often we refuse to let them go. We are like the

Shulammite maiden who wants to camp out in the lower places. We know we are saved, and so we are content with that.

Review this memory verse:

> *No discipline seems pleasant at the time, but painful. Later on, however, it produces a harvest of righteousness and peace for those who have been trained by it.* (Hebrews 12:11)

21. Kathy compared disciplining ourselves to changing the course of a river. It means work. It means carrying rocks to redirect the flow. It takes commitment and persistency. But, in time, the river begins to move another way, and then it begins to make a channel. It then becomes a place of rejoicing. Have you had success in redirecting any rivers? If so, share what you have learned, especially in the context of Hebrews 12:11.

    _____

    _____

    _____

22. Review the journey of the Shulammite maiden, comparing it to your own.

    A. Describe some of her feelings in her first-love time. (Songs of Songs 1:2–4 and 2:3–6)

    _____

    _____

    B. What does her lover ask of her? Where is she hiding, and what does this represent spiritually? (Song of Songs 2:10–14)

    _____

    _____

    C. Where do you tend to camp out, to hide, in the lower places?

    _____

    _____

    D. When her lover leaves her to go to the higher places alone, describe her pain in this wilderness time. Describe also his grace toward her. (Song of Songs 2:17–3:4)

    _____

    _____

E. How has Jesus shown you grace when you have camped out in the lower places?

_____

_____

F. What refrain do you find in Song of Songs 4:6 that is similar to what you saw in Song of Songs 2:17? What significant difference do you find?

_____

_____

G. How does the lover respond to the Shulammite this time? (Song of Songs 4:7) What is the significance spiritually?

_____

_____

H. Describe a time when you have felt Jesus' pleasure with you.

_____

_____

I. Describe the growth you see in the Shulammite maiden. (Song of Songs 4:16) What is the significance of this spiritually?

_____

_____

J. Describe the invincible-love stage in her life. (Song of Songs 8:6–7)

_____

_____

23. Sometimes the Lord takes us through the wilderness, not because of sin, but to strengthen our faith. Review the wilderness journey of Mary and Martha of Bethany.

A. What reasons does Jesus give for allowing His loved ones to walk through the wilderness? (John 11:4 and 11:14)

_____

_____

B. What lessons can you learn from Martha's experience in the wilderness? (John 11:21–27 and 11:38–41)

C. What lessons can you learn from Mary's experience in the wilderness? (John 11:28–35)

_____

_____

D. What did you learn about the power of God? (John 11:41–44)

_____

_____

E. Are you wandering through a wilderness presently? How can you apply any of these lessons?

_____

_____

Review this memory verse:

> *Even though I walk*
> *through the valley of the shadow of death,*
> *I will fear no evil,*
> *for you are with me;*
> *your rod and your staff,*
> *they comfort me.* (Psalm 23:4)

DAY 5

Our Love Is Here to Stay

In marriage, it takes time to trust the heart of your husband. In the early years you are more apt to be hurt by a remark, because you don't completely trust his heart and he doesn't completely know what you need. But if you hang on and continue to love, you are most likely to make it through the wilderness into the land of invincible love. Then, when trouble comes, it doesn't destroy your love, because you know your husband's heart and he knows yours.

In the same way, it takes time to trust the heart of God, for He often acts in mysterious ways. He may allow injury for our own good. But even in the darkest of days, if we get quiet enough, He will come. He will play the music.

And when we trust Him, when we abandon ourselves to Him, as we have seen the individuals do whom we have studied, we move into the land of invincible love. This is not a land that is free of pain, but it is a land of peace and confidence. It is also a place where the love of God is so strong that it bubbles up, like a fountain, and overflows to others. That's what we saw in the lives of Mary, the mother of Jesus, of Ruth, of the Shulammite maiden, and of Mary of Bethany.

Mary, the mother of Jesus, was ready to risk everything: her reputation, her engagement, and her safety. She said, "I am the Lord's servant. . . . May it be to me as you have said" (Luke 1:38).

The risks Ruth took were amazing, leaving her land, her family, her gods. But somehow she had become persuaded that Naomi's God could be trusted. And so she surrendered all.

The Shulammite maiden left her hiding place and went to the "mountain of myrrh."

Likewise, the risk Mary of Bethany took was astonishing. Women were supposed to stay in the background. Yet Mary of Bethany boldly entered a house full of men. It didn't matter to her that she was risking her pride, her reputation, and her dowry—she was ready to abandon all for Jesus.

To prepare your heart today, reflect on a Bible verse or a passage from a favorite book, or you may even choose to break into a joyful song.

Review this memory verse:

> *I have been crucified with Christ and I no longer live, but Christ lives in me. The life I live in the body, I live by faith in the Son of God, who loved me and gave himself for me.* (Galatians 2:20)

24. Review Mary of Bethany's invincible-love scene.

   A. Describe Mary's act. (John 12:3)

   _____

   _____

The perfume's fragrance filled the whole house and lingered, no doubt, on Jesus through the following holy week, through His crucifixion, and on His body in the grave. Mary of Bethany turned that day into a day that would go down in history. Kathy has often prayed:

Jesus,
  teach me to kneel
    at Your feet.
  to talk with You,
    watch You,
      hear You,
        worship You,

  so that
    my prayers and praise
    are like that costly ointment
  and all of heaven
    filled with the fragrance
      of our time together.

B. As Mary brought delight to Jesus, do you feel you are bringing Him delight in your worship? Are you growing in this area? Explain.

_____

_____

C. Describe how Jesus defended Mary. (John 12:7–8 and Mark 14:6–9)

_____

_____

D. Are you growing in your desire to seek the praise of God rather than the praise of man? Explain.

_____

_____

E. Jesus said, "She did what she could" (Mark 14:8a). Are you growing in your ability to seize the moment and to do what you can? Explain.

_____

_____

25. Review how, even in the most difficult of times, the Lord "played the music" for Naomi.

A. How did He play it, initially, through the friendship of Ruth? (Ruth 1:16–17 and 2:2)

_____

_____

B. Describe the point at which Naomi finally heard the music. (Ruth 2:18–20) Why do you think she was finally able to hear it?

_____

_____

C. How did God continue to play the music for Naomi? (Ruth 3:16–18 and 4:13–15)

_____

_____

D. How has the Lord "played the music" for you in this study, _Falling in Love with Jesus?_

_____

_____

Review this memory verse:

> _Many waters cannot quench love;_
> _rivers cannot wash it away._ (Song of Songs 8:7a)

Horatio Spafford lost three daughters at sea. He asked to see the place where they died. Afterward he went back to his cabin and penned the lyrics that have ministered to so many. Meditate on them or, if you like, sing them to the Lord.

> When peace, like a river, attendeth my way,
> When sorrows like sea-billows roll;
> Whatever my lot, Thou hast taught me to say,
> It is well, it is well with my soul.
>
> It is well . . . with my soul. . . .
> It is well, it is well, with my soul.
>
> And, Lord, haste the day when the faith shall be sight,
> The clouds be rolled back as a scroll,
> The trump shall resound and the Lord shall descend,
> "Even so"—it is well with my soul.
>
> It is well . . . with my soul. . . .
> It is well, it is well, with my soul.

Finale

REVIEW

26. In a year, what do you think you will still remember from this study? What is your "takeaway"? How have you been changed? (Hear from as many women as wish to share.)

_____

_____

_____

PRAYER

Spend some time in praise for ways the Lord has "kissed" you in this study. Close by singing "I Love You, Lord" (see Appendix A).

Appendix A
Song Lyrics

AND CAN IT BE THAT I SHOULD GAIN?
(Charles Wesley)

And can it be that I should gain
An interest in the Saviour's blood
Died He for me who caused His pain
For me who Him to death pursued
Amazing love, how can it be
That Thou my God shouldst die for me
Amazing love, how can it be
That Thou my God shouldst die for me

He left His Father's throne above
So free, so infinite His grace
Emptied Himself of all but love
And bled for Adam's helpless race
Tis mercy all immense and free
For O, my God it found out me
Amazing love, how can it be
That Thou my God shouldst die for me

AMAZING GRACE
(John Newton)

Amazing grace how sweet the sound
That saved a wretch like me
I once was lost but now am found
Was blind but now I see

'Twas grace that taught my heart to fear
And grace my fears relieved
How precious did that grace appear
The hour I first believed

Thro' many dangers toils and snares
I have already come
Tis grace hath bro't me safe thus far
And grace will lead me home

When we've been there ten thousand years
Bright shining as the sun
We've no less days to sing God's praise
Than when we first begun

GREAT IS THY FAITHFULNESS
(Thomas O. Chisholm)

Great is Thy faithfulness, O God my Father
There is no shadow of turning with Thee
Thou changest not, Thy compassions they
fail not
As Thou hast been Thou forever wilt be

(chorus)
Great is Thy faithfulness
Great is Thy faithfulness
Morning by morning new mercies I see
All I have needed Thy hand hath provided
Great is Thy faithfulness
Lord unto me

Summer and winter and springtime and
harvest
Sun moon and stars in their courses above
Join with all nature in manifold witness
To Thy great faithfulness mercy and love

(repeat chorus)

Pardon for sin and a peace that endureth
Thy own dear presence to cheer and to
guide
Strength for today and bright hope for
tomorrow
Blessings all mind with ten thousand beside

(repeat chorus)

I LOVE YOU, LORD
(Laurie Klein)
I love You, Lord,
And I lift my voice
To worship You
O my soul rejoice
Take joy, my King
In what You hear
May it be a sweet, sweet sound
In Your ear

CHANGE MY HEART, O GOD
(Eddie Espinosa)

Change my heart, O God
Make it ever true
Change my heart, O God
May I be like You
You are the Potter
I am the clay
Mold me and make me
This is what I pray
Change my heart, O God
Make it ever true
Change my heart, O God
May I be like You

OPEN OUR EYES, LORD
(Robert Cull)

Open our eyes, Lord
We want to see Jesus
To reach out and touch Him
And say that we love Him
Open our ears, Lord
And help us to listen
Open our eyes, Lord
We want to see Jesus

JESUS, NAME ABOVE ALL NAMES
(Naida Hearn)

Jesus, name above all names
Beautiful Savior glorious Lord
Emanuel God is with us
Blessed Redeemer Living Word

YOU ARE STILL HOLY
(Rita Springer)

Holy, You are still holy
Even when the darkness surrounds my life
Sovereign, You are still sovereign
Even when confusion has blinded my eyes
Lord I don't deserve Your kind affection
When my unbelief has kept me from Your
touch
I want my life to be a pure reflection of
Your love

And so I come into Your chamber and I
dance at Your feet Lord
You are my Savior and I'm at Your mercy
All that has been in my life up till now
It belongs to You
You are still holy

Holy, You are still holy
Even though I don't understand Your ways
Sovereign, You will be sovereign
Even when my circumstances don't change
Lord, I don't deserve Your tender patience
When my unbelief has kept me from Your
truth
I want my life to be a sweet devotion to You

Appendix B
Memory Verses

Week 1

As a bridegroom rejoices over his bride,
so will your God rejoice over you.
—Isaiah 62:5b

Week 2

The LORD your God is with you,
he is mighty to save.
He will take great delight in you,
he will quiet you with his love,
he will rejoice over you with singing.
—Zephaniah 3:17

Week 3

Above all else, guard your heart,
for it is the wellspring of life.
—Proverbs 4:23

Week 4

Entreat me not to leave thee, or to return from following after thee: for whither thou goest, I will go; and where thou lodgest, I will lodge: thy people shall be my people, and thy God my God:

Where thou diest, will I die, and there will I be buried: the LORD do so to me, and more also, if ought but death part thee and me.
—Ruth 1:16–17 (KJV)

Week 5

Let him kiss me with the kisses of his mouth—
for your love is more delightful than wine.

—Song of Songs 1:2

Week 6

No discipline seems pleasant at the time, but
painful. Later on, however, it produces a harvest of righteousness and peace for those who
have been trained by it.

—Hebrews 12:11

Week 7

Even though I walk
 through the valley of the shadow of death,
I will fear no evil,
 for you are with me;
your rod and your staff,
 they comfort me.

—Psalm 23:4

Week 8

I have been crucified with Christ and I no
longer live, but Christ lives in me. The life I
live in the body, I live by faith in the Son of
God, who loved me and gave himself for me.

—Galatians 2:20

Week 9

Many waters cannot quench love;
 rivers cannot wash it away.

—Song of Songs 8:7a

Appendix C
Kisses from the King

A "kiss from the King" can be a living word of prophecy (a scripture that particularly ministers to you in a time of need), a provision (an answer to prayer or an unexpected blessing), or a sense of His presence in times of joy, pain, or worship. Recording His kisses and reflecting on them helps keep your love alive. It is also important to ask for His kisses.

Let him kiss me with the kisses of his mouth—
for your love is more delightful than wine.
—Song of Songs 1:2

Kiss (Date): _____

Kiss (Date): _____

Kiss (Date): _____

Kiss (Date): _____

Kiss (Date): _____

Kiss (Date): _____

Kiss (Date): _____

Kiss (Date): _____

Kiss (Date): _____

Kiss (Date): _____

Kiss (Date): _____

Kiss (Date): _____

Kiss (Date): _____

Kiss (Date): _____

Kiss (Date): _____

Kiss (Date): _____

Kiss (Date): _____

Kiss (Date): _____

Kiss (Date): _____

Kiss (Date): _____

Kiss (Date): _____

Kiss (Date): _____

Kiss (Date): _____

Kiss (Date): _____

Kiss (Date): _____

Kiss (Date): _____

Kiss (Date): _____

Kiss (Date): _____

Kiss (Date): _____

Kiss (Date): _____

Kiss (Date): _____

Kiss (Date): _____

Kiss (Date): _____

Kiss (Date): _____

Kiss (Date): _____

Kiss (Date): _____

Kiss (Date): _____

Kiss (Date): _____

Kiss (Date): _____

Kiss (Date): _____

Kiss (Date): _____

Kiss (Date): _____

Kiss (Date): _____

Kiss (Date): _____

Kiss (Date): _____

Kiss (Date): _____

Appendix D
Movie Night!

Make this a fun night with popcorn, and start early, because *Camelot* is a long movie and you'll want lots of time to talk afterward. Have candles or a blazing fire for romance as you consider how this musical is a parable for many of the themes you have studied in *Falling in Love with Jesus*.

Your discussion leader, or someone she delegates, will plan ahead to rent or buy the Warner Brother's musical production of *Camelot*, starring Vanessa Redgrave as Guenevere. (It can be found in the "Classics" or "Musicals" section at many bigger video stores. It contains two tapes and is rated G.)

BEFORE YOU WATCH

Learning to look at some of the classic love stories as parables for falling in love with Jesus can have a dramatic impact on your thought life. Remember, as in all parables, not all of the details work, yet the central message works very well—so we will concentrate on that.

Expulsion of Adam and Eve from Paradise
MASACCIO (TOMMASO DI GIOVANNI) (1401–1428)[xiv]

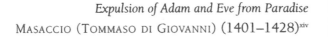

This famous painting captures the depth of pain we bring
on ourselves when we betray the heart of God.

Just as paradise was lost by the betrayal of Adam and Eve,
Camelot was lost by the betrayal of Lancelot and Guenevere.
Sin looked so good, and was sweet for a while. But the pain
and the cost that followed were unimaginably high.

In this classic love triangle, King Arthur is our Christ figure. He is kind and noble and good. Guenevere, who becomes his bride, loves him deeply. Guenevere represents us. We are loved and we love the Lord, but we have a tendency toward betrayal. From the very beginning you will see how Guenevere wants continual excitement and fails to appreciate what she has. Yet despite these flaws, which King Arthur sees, he loves her and is very good to her.

Note also how terribly attractive sin is, and how deceitful. Finally, note the tremendous cost of Guenevere's sin and the rippling consequences. In many ways, Sir Lancelot and Guenevere, who betrayed King Arthur, are reminiscent of another couple who betrayed the heart of God.

As you watch

Consider what led to the fall. May it be a parable to help you to guard your heart.

Some may be offended by the storyline that involves Merlin, the magician. We were not, because this is a fairy tale and because authors as esteemed as C. S. Lewis and J. R. R. Tolkien have used such characters. But you may have to give grace in this area or others.

If you do not have time to watch the whole movie and have the discussion, watch through the song "What Do the Simple Folk Do?"

Discussion questions

1. As *Camelot* opens, King Arthur is in great pain. He asks, "Where did I go wrong?" "How did it happen?" "Should I not have loved her?" So often we don't think about how running after other loves breaks the heart of God, but it does. Read the Lord's heartbreak in Hosea 11:3–4 and 11:8. What similarities do you see with King Arthur?

2. What flaw did you see in Guenevere as she sang "Where Are the Simple Joys of Maidenhood?" and "The Lusty Month of May"? Do you see this flaw in yourself? Why do we have a tendency to make light of sin? The world winks at sexual immorality, gluttony, cheating on taxes, lying, etc. Why is it dangerous to see sin as "no big deal"?

3. Describe the love of King Arthur for Guenevere. Describe his strategy for how to handle a woman. How did he live it out?

4. Describe the sweetness of the first-love time between Arthur and Guenevere. Describe her arrival, on horseback, to Camelot. Describe their wedding and the early days when they planned the round table. How did their love impact the world around them for good?

5. When your relationship with the Lord is right, when you are walking purely before Him, how does it impact you? How does it impact others?

6. Lancelot was a godly man, but he too had a flaw. What do you think it was? Read Proverbs 16:18 and 1 Corinthians 10:12. What could you learn from this?

7. So often we associate infidelity with an unhappy marriage, but that is often not

the case. In the Lord we have the perfect Bridegroom, even more amazing than King Arthur. And yet we betray Him. Why? Review the following:

> What I (Kathy) sense in myself and what I've sensed as I've talked to believers on the road is that we get impatient. We don't feel like there is enough immediate payback. We're lonely, we may be facing some kind of wilderness experience, and we don't want to wait for God to fill our needs. So we settle for a temporary filling. I have a friend who has recently left a homosexual lifestyle. She said, "I've got to tell you, I miss the high. I miss the camaraderie. I miss the titillation of it." My friend has stayed pure because she's hanging on to God and His promises, and she knows if she returns to her old life it is just going to be a quick fix with a false peace and then all will come crashing down. But it can be lonely waiting on God. It's like the Lazarus story. Jesus stayed where He was for two days, and Mary and Martha were thinking, *Are You there? Do You care?*
>
> We are so easily deceived. It is like grabbing the tail of a snake. He will turn on us, overpowering us. If we try to restrain him and put him back in his box, he will refuse to be restrained. He is a "viper," Jonathan Edwards says, who hisses and spits at God (footnote omitted).

Why do you think Guenevere and Lancelot betrayed King Arthur? How were they deceived?

8. How did the consequences of their sin have a ripple effect? If they had gone to King Arthur early on, confessed, and repented, the story might have turned out very differently. Why do you think they didn't do this? When we cling to sinful ways, how are we being deceived?

9. Describe some of the consequences of their sin to themselves. Consider their song "I Loved You Once in Silence." Consider the consequences to others.

10. Recall the scene in which Guenevere and King Arthur try to bring joy back to their lives and sing "What Do the Simple Folk Do?" How effective were their remedies? What does this teach you that you could apply personally in your life?

11. When you consider this parable, what strengthens you personally? Be specific.

Notes

Chapter 1: A Dream Is a Wish Your Heart Makes

1. John D. W. Watts, "Isaiah 34–66," in *Word Biblical Commentary*, ed. David A. Hubbard, Glenn W. Barker, and John D. W. Watts (Nashville: W Publishing Group, 1987), 25:313.
2. Philip Yancey, *Disappointment with God* (Grand Rapids: Zondervan, 1988), 94.
3. Mary Blye Howe, "The Love of God Is the Lover's Passionate Embrace," *Dallas Morning News*, 5 February, 2000, 5G.
4. Max Lucado, *Just Like Jesus* (Nashville: W Publishing Group, 1998), 3.

Chapter 2: Someday My Prince Will Come

1. Luci Shaw, "Made Flesh." in *The Risk of Birth: A Gift Book of Christ-Poems* (Wheaton, Ill.: Harold Shaw, 1974), 28.
2. Dallas Willard, *The Divine Conspiracy: Rediscovering Our Hidden Life in God* (New York: HarperCollins, 1998), 113.
3. Brent Curtis and John Eldredge, *The Sacred Romance: Drawing Closer to the Heart of God* (Nashville: Thomas Nelson, 1997), 6–7.
4. *The Metropolitan Tabernacle Pulpit: Sermons Preached and Revised by C. H. Spurgeon, During the Year 1863* (Pasadena, Tex.: Pilgrim Pulbications, 1970), 9:385.
5. *Evangelical Dictionary of Theology*, ed. Walter A. Elwell (Grand Rapids: Baker, 1984), 499.
6. Willard, *The Divine Conspiracy*, 36–37.
7. John Piper, *Desiring God: Meditations of a Christian Hedonist* (Sisters, Ore.: Multnomah, 1996), 66.
8. Pastor Mike Lano, Sermon to the Trinity Presbyterian Church of Kearney, Nebraska, October 2, 2000.
9. Joni Eareckson Tada and Stephen Estes, *When God Weeps: Why Our Sufferings Matter to the Almighty* (Grand Rapids: Zondervan, 1997), 56.
10. Kathy Troccoli, adapted from *My Life Is in Your Hands* (Grand Rapids: Zondervan, 1997), 162–64.

Chapter 3: Looking for Love in All the Wrong Places

1. Philip Yancey, *The Bible Jesus Read* (Grand Rapids: Zondervan, 1999), 159.
2. Ibid., 159–60.
3. Gail Sheehy, *Passages* (New York: E. P. Dutton and Co., 1974), 6.
4. Jonathan Edwards, as quoted in Curtis and Eldredge, *The Sacred Romance*, 133.
5. *Compton's Interactive Bible: New International Version*, "Chemosh" (Cambridge: Compton's NewMedia, 1996).
6. John Eldredge, *The Journey of Desire: Searching for the Life We've Only Dreamed Of* (Nashville: Thomas Nelson, 2000), 129–30, 134.
7. C. S. Lewis, *Mere Christianity* (New York: MacMillan, 1958), 3.
8. James D. G. Dunn, "Romans 1–8," in *Word Biblical Commentary*, ed. David A. Hubbard, Glenn W. Barker, and Ralph P. Martin (Nashville: W Publishing Group, 1988), 38a:71.
9. Ibid., 59.
10. Eldredge, *The Journey of Desire*, 35.
11. A. W. Tozer, *The Pursuit of God* (Harrisburg: Christian Publications, 1948), 14.
12. Ibid., 14–15.
13. Ibid., 15.
14. Yancey, *The Bible Jesus Read*, 115.

Chapter 4: It Had to Be You

1. David C. and Esther R. Gross, *Under the Wedding Canopy: Love & Marriage in Judaism* (New York: Hippocreme Books, 1996), 59.
2. Elisabeth Elliot, *Let Me Be a Woman: Notes to My Daughter on the Meaning of Womanhood* (Wheaton, Ill.: Tyndale, 1986), 13.

3. Gene Edwards, *The Divine Romance* (Wheaton, Ill.: Tyndale, 1993), n.p.
4. Christopher Wordsworth, as quoted in Charles Spurgeon, *The Treasury of David,* vol. 3, pt. 2. (Peabody, Mass.: Hendrickson, n.d.), 90.
5. Spurgeon, *The Treasury of David,* 263.
6. Darrell L. Bock, *Luke* (Grand Rapids: Baker, 1996), 2(9:51–24:53): 1275, 1273.
7. T. W. Manson, as quoted in Bock, *Luke,* 1278.
8. Bock, *Luke,* 1284–85.
9. Jan Silvious, *Fool-Proofing Your Life: Wisdom for Untangling Your Most Difficult Relationships* (Colorado Springs: WaterBrook, 1998), 52.
10. Max Lucado, *When Christ Comes: The Beginning of the Very Best* (Nashville: W Publishing Group, 1999), 145.
11. Andrew Murray, *Like Christ* (Minneapolis: Bethany, 1974), 53.

Chapter 5: Love Me Tender
1. Sheldon Vanauken, *A Severe Mercy* (New York: Harper & Row, 1977), 25–26, 29.
2. Ibid., 28–29.
3. Charles Spurgeon, "Sermon 636," in *The C. H. Spurgeon Collection* CD ROM (Rio, Wiss.: AGES Software, 1998).
4. Matthew Henry, "Job to Song of Solomon," in *Matthew Henry's Commentary on the Whole Bible* (Peabody, Mass.: Hendrickson, 1991), 3:867.
5. Joseph Irons, as quoted in Spurgeon, "Sermon 282," in *The C. H. Spurgeon Collection.*
6. Spurgeon, "Sermon 282," in *The C .H. Spurgeon Collection.*
7. Dwight L. Moody, as quoted in Watchman Nee, *Song of Songs,* trans. Elizabeth K. Mei and Daniel Smith (Fort Washington, Penn.: Christian Literature Crusade, 1965), 38.
8. Nee, *Song of Songs,* 17.
9. Jamie Lash, *A Kiss a Day* (Hagerstown, Md.: Ebed, 1996), 17.
10. Bruce Wilkinson, *The Prayer of Jabez: Breaking through to the Blessed Life* (Sisters, Ore.: Multnomah, 2000), 27.
11. Spurgeon, *The Treasury of David,* vol. 3. pt. 1, 173.
12. C. S. Lewis, *Reflections on the Psalms* (New York: Harcourt, Brace and Word, 1958), 56.
13. Richard Sibbes, as quoted in Spurgeon, *The Treasury of David,* vol. 3, pt. 1, 244.
14. Lash, *A Kiss a Day,* 31.
15. Bock, *Luke* (Grand Rapids: Baker, 1993), 1(1:1–9:50):1040.
16. Walter Wangerin, Jr., *The Book of God: The Bible as a Novel* (Grand Rapids: Zondervan, 1996), 741.
17. Charles Swindoll, *Insight for Living* radio broadcast.
18. Curtis and Eldredge, *The Sacred Romance,* 6.

Chapter 6: Killing Me Softly
1. Hannah Hurnard, *Hinds' Feet on High Places* (Wheaton, Ill.: Tyndale, 1977), 62–63.
   Unfortunately, after Hannah Hurnard wrote this wonderful classic, she turned away from Christianity into universalism, pantheism, and New Age philosophies. We cannot recommend her subsequent books. However, *Hinds' Feet in High Places* adheres to the Word of God and is a beautiful and true allegory.
2. Ibid., 66.
3. Charles Spurgeon, *Spurgeon's Sermons* (Grand Rapids: Baker, 1996), 9:330.
4. Nee, *Song of Songs,* 60–61.
5. Jackie Rodriguez, "The Kisses of the King," *Spirit Led Woman,* August/September 1999, 26.
6. Luis Palau, *The Schemer and the Dreamer: God's Way to the Top* (Grand Rapids: Discovery House, 1999), 9.
7. Leslie Williams, *Night Wrestlings: Struggling for Answers and Finding God* (Nashville: W Publishing Group, 1997), 14.
8. Francine Rivers, *Redeeming Love* (Chicago: Alabaster, 1997), 81.
9. Leslie Williams, *Seduction of the Lesser Gods: Life, Love, Church, and Other Dangerous Idols* (Nashville: Word, 1997), 12.
10. Ruth Bell Graham, as quoted in Janet Kobobel Grant, *Experiencing God's Presence,* ed. Traci Mullins (Grand Rapids: Zondervan, 1998), 50.

Chapter 7: You Can't Hurry Love

1. Barbara Brown Taylor, *The Preaching Life* (Cambridge: Cowley, 1993), 141.
2. Spurgeon, "Sermon 995," in *The C. H. Spurgeon Collection*.
3. Lewis, *Mere Christianity*, 41.
4. Charles Spurgeon, *Spurgeon's Expository Encyclopedia: Sermons by Charles H. Spurgeon,* (Grand Rapids: Baker, 1998), 3:455.
5. H. R. Reynolds, "John," in *The Pulpit Commentary*, ed. H. D. M. Spence and Joseph S. Excell, vol. 17, pt. 2 (Peabody, Mass.: Hendrickson, n.d.), 91.
6. Elisabeth Elliot, *The Path of Loneliness* (Nashville: Thomas Nelson, 1991), 22.

Chapter 8: Unforgettable

1. Debby Jones and Jackie Kendall, *Lady in Waiting: Developing Your Love Relationships* (Shippensburg, Penn.: Treasure House, 1995), 3.
2. Leon Morris, "John," in *The New International Commentary* (Grand Rapids: Eerdmans, 1971), 576–77.
3. A. B. Bruce, *The Training of the Twelve* (Grand Rapids: Kregel, 1988), 301.
4. Bock, *Luke*, 1:695.
5. Walter Wangerin, Jr., as quoted by Bruce Bursma, *The Chicago Tribune*, 8 August, 1986.
6. Willard, *The Divine Conspiracy*, 77.
7. Reynolds, *The Pulpit Commentary*, 270.
8. Spurgeon, "Sermon 2475," in *The C. H. Spurgeon Collection*.
9. Nee, *Song of Songs*, 84–85.

Chapter 9: Our Love Is Here to Stay

1. Dr. Henry Cloud and Dr. John Townsend, *Boundaries* (Grand Rapids: Zondervan, 1992), 161–62.
2. J. Vernon McGee, *Ruth: The Romance of Redemption* (Grand Rapids: Zondervan, 1953), 88–83.
3. Cyril J. Barber, *Ruth: An Expositional Commentary* (Chicago: Moody, 1983), 101.

Chapter 10: All Is Well

1. Yancey, *Disappointment with God*, 94.
2. Vanauken, *A Severe Mercy*, 28–29.

Illustration Sources

i.   *Great Women of the Bible in Art and Literature* (Grand Rapids: Eerdmans, 1993), 249.

ii.   Carlo Pietrangeli, *Painting in the Vatican* (Boston: Bulfish Press, 1996), 452.

iii. *Great Women of the Bible in Art and Literature,* 246.

iv.   Ibid., 250.

v.   Keith J. White, *Masterpieces of the Bible: Insights into Classical Art of Faith* (Grand Rapids: Baker, 1997), 35.

vi.   *Great Women of the Bible in Art and Literature,* 157.

vii. Bruce Bernard, *The Bible and Its Painters* (New York: Macmillan, 1983), 189.

viii. *Great Women of the Bible in Art and Literature,* 273.

ix.   Ibid., 69.

x.   Bernard, *The Bible and Its Painters,* 58.

xi.   http://sunsitedk/cgfa/dore/p-dore/.html

xii. Bernard, *The Bible and Its Painters,* 199.

xiii. Ibid., 155.

xiv. Ibid., 29.

Sources for Songs

"And Can It Be That I Should Gain?"
Public domain.

"Amazing Grace"
Public domain.

"Great Is Thy Faithfulness"
Public domain.

"It Is Well with My Soul"
Public domain.

"I Love You, Lord"
Lyrics by Laurie Klein. Copyright © 1978 House of Mercy Music. Administered by Maranatha Music. All rights reserved. Used by permission.

"Change My Heart, O God"
Lyrics by Eddie Espinosa. Copyright © 1982 Mercy/Vineyard Publishing (ASCAP). All rights reserved. Used by permission.

"Open Our Eyes, Lord"
Lyrics by Robert Cull. Copyright © 1976 Maranatha Music. All rights reserved. Used by permission.

"Jesus, Name above All Names"
Lyrics by Naida Hearn. Copyright © 1974 Scripture in Song (a division of Integrity Music, Inc.). All rights reserved. Used by permission.

"You Are Still Holy"
Lyrics by Rita Springer. Copyright © 1998 Vineyard Worship Publishing USA. Administered by Mercy/Vineyard Publishing/BMI. All rights reserved. Used by permission.

"Missing You"
Lyrics by Chris Rice. Copyright © 1994 BMG songs, Inc. (ASCAP). All rights reserved. Used by permission.

"Help Myself to You"
Lyrics by Kathy Troccoli. Copyright ©1991 BMG Songs, Inc. (ASCAP). All rights reserved. Used by permission.

"Break My Heart"
Lyrics by Kathy Troccoli. Copyright © 2000 Sony/ATV Songs LLC/BMI. All rights on behalf of Sony/ATV Songs LLC administered by Sony/ATV Music Publishing, 8 Music Square West, Nashville, TN 37203. All rights reserved. Used by permission.

"May I Be His Love"
Lyrics by Kathy Troccoli and Madeline Stone. Copyright © 1995 Sony/ATV Songs LLC and We Care Music. All rights on behalf of Sony/ATV Songs LLC administered by Sony/ATV Music Publishing, 8 Music Square West, Nashville, TN 37203., All rights reserved. Used by persmission.